Everybody Wins

BY ARTHUR MILLER

PLAYS

All My Sons
Death of a Salesman
An Enemy of the People (*adaptation*)
The Crucible
A Memory of Two Mondays
A View from the Bridge
After the Fall
Incident at Vichy
The Price
The Creation of the World and Other Business
The Archbishop's Ceiling
The American Clock
Two-way Mirror
Danger: Memory!

SCREENPLAYS

The Misfits
Playing for Time
Everybody Wins

FICTION

Focus (*novel*)
I Don't Need You Any More (*stories*)
Jane's Blanket (*for children*)

NONFICTION

Situation Normal
"Salesman" in Beijing
Timebends: A Life

WITH INGE MORATH

In Russia
In the Country
Chinese Encounters

COLLECTIONS

Arthur Miller's Collected Plays
The Portable Arthur Miller
The Theater Essays of Arthur Miller

Everybody Wins

A SCREENPLAY BY

ARTHUR MILLER

with a preface by the author

GROVE WEIDENFELD
New York

Published by Grove Weidenfeld
A division of Wheatland Corporation
841 Broadway
New York, NY 10003-4793

Published in Canada by General Publishing Company, Ltd.

Library of Congress Cataloging-in-Publication Data
Miller, Arthur, 1915-
    Everybody wins: a screenplay/Arthur Miller.—1st ed.
        p.   cm.
    ISBN 0-8021-3200-6 (pbk.: alk. paper)
    I. Title.
PN1997.E93   1989
791.43′72—dc20   89-17050
                                                        CIP

Manufactured in the United States of America

Printed on acid-free paper

Designed by Irving Perkins Associates

First Edition 1990

10 9 8 7 6 5 4 3 2 1

PREFACE
On Screenwriting and Language

A funny thing happens to screenplays on the way to the screen. It isn't simply that they get changed, subtly or otherwise, from their earlier incarnations, but that they become brittle. This is only true for the writer, of course. He misses the lines that were merely shadings of meaning and would probably hold things up in a movie, which, after all, has to *move*. But in the final version of *Everybody Wins,* compared to earlier drafts, surprisingly little of the basic material was altered, although I agreed to cut a few scenes and revise the ending. In general, what I think happened—and this is probably usual in moviemaking—is that suggestion through words became rather more blatant indication through images.

I hasten to add that this is not a gripe, if only because it is, in my view, a generic quality of the form. A description in words tends to inflate, expand, and inflame the imagination, so that in the end the thing or person described is amplified into a larger-than-life figment. But something photographed is lifted out of the imagination and becomes simply what it really is, or less. It is montage rather than the actual photograph itself that gives the impression of an imaginary world larger than life. Words, unable to imitate reality, must in their nature serve it up in metaphoric guise, but film gives us the appearance of reality directly.

If a telephone is photographed, isolated on a table, and the camera is left running, it becomes more and more what it is—a telephone in all its detail. Andy Warhol let the camera run on the Empire State Building for maybe an hour or more. I left before the "end" of this picture, so I'm not sure how long it lasted, but in the twenty minutes I watched, it never to my mind rose to metaphor, simply remaining what it was—the Empire State Building.

Things go differently on a stage. Set a phone on a table under a light and raise the curtain, and in complete silence, after a few minutes, something will accrete around it. Questions and anticipations will begin to emanate from it, we will begin to imagine meanings in its isolation—in a word, the phone becomes an incipient metaphor. Possibly because we cannot see its detail as sharply as on film or because it is surrounded by a much greater space, it begins to animate, to take on suggestive possibilities, very nearly a kind of self-consciousness. Something of the same is true of words as opposed to images. The word is not and can't be any more than suggestive of an idea or sensation; it *is* nothing in itself.

There is always too much dialogue. And it's true, there is, for one thing because dialogue cannot be seen. The contradiction, I suppose, is that movies—most of them, anyway—require a writer's sense of form while inherently rejecting his word-love. And so the writer, accustomed to forming sentences on which all his effects rely, ends up with something truncated and not quite his own on paper; with luck, however, it is paradoxically more his own on the screen. For it turns out—if he is lucky with director and actors—that the meaning of his lost lines is actually visible in pictures. I think that the quality of the final work is rougher and cruder, more brutally telegraphic, than when it was action described in words. But again, the word made flesh may *be* more and suggest less. It is a very mysterious business, and by no means a simple question of better or worse, but of differences of aesthetic feeling, of timbre and tissue, that always accompany differences of form. One need only recall the innumerable fine novels that simply could not be made to work on the screen because the quality of their language was removed; their story-essence vanished when their language was discarded.

Among "real" writers—novelists, playwrights, poets—
screenwriting, when it is not regarded as a cousin of engi-
neering, is seen as an art on a par with clothing design; the
product has no life of its own until it is occupied by the
wearer. I am afraid that this, at least in my view, is truer than
one would wish, but it is necessary to add that there have been
many more significant films over the past twenty-five years
than plays or, proportionately, even novels. Nevertheless,
screenplays, especially the good ones that work, tend by the
nature of the art to be self-effacing, vanishing, as it were, into
the total impression of the film, this in contrast to the play,
which in the Western tradition has been assimilated to litera-
ture as a respectable form apart from performance (something that was not yet the case as late as Elizabethan times,
when playscripts were tossed to managers and actors without
reaching print). Except among technicians, the screenplay
has little or no existence unless filmed, and the few excep-
tions, like Pinter's unproduced work for the screen, are precisely that—isolated examples that illuminate the rule.

The screenplay is the first element in a collaborative art,
but only an element for all that, and not, like a stage play, a
thing in itself. It is a sort of libretto for camera, its energies
moving outward to serve the other elements in the film and
to organize them for a common purpose. The forces in and
around the stage play, in contrast, move in the opposite
direction, for it is the play that is to be served—by director,
actors, designer, costumer. An opera libretto is likewise con-
tent not to be noticed by the public, even as the singers and
conductor know that it is their vital support, without which
the music would fail to fly out to the audience's ear.

The screenplay may do many things, but one thing it must
do, and that is give meaning to the pictures. In this sense it is
equivalent to the words in a cartoon balloon or the titles
sometimes given photographs or paintings. These may ori-
ent us as to the time and place a photo was shot or a picture

painted, but there can't be many photos or paintings made memorable by their labels and dates. Indeed, the vitality of a screenplay, indispensable as it is to the finished film, springs from the life-giving structure by which the order of the images—the film's most affecting element—is organized.

The very invisibility of the screenplay accounts for the screenwriter's anonymity before the audience and most critics. To be sure, he alone was there when the pages were blank, it was his godlike hand that gave form to dust, but his occasional smart or touching line of dialogue notwithstanding, it isn't really words that people come to hear or long remember; it is actors and their mannerisms, their noses and hair and tones of voice, that really matter to them. And ironically, the more authority the actor has in performing his role, the further from sight the screenwriter recedes; in effect, the actor has eaten him. Indeed, when this happens, the movie is successful, since the actor seems to have originated his lines.

Except for the money, when there is any, screenwriting is a rather thankless profession compared with other forms of writing. The film medium belongs essentially to the director, its attraction for the public will always be the actor, and there will never be a way around that. There cannot be a Eugene O'Neill of the movies. Every element and person in the enterprise exists to serve the director's central purpose, which is to make the actors seem believable.

This may be why the most persuasive film acting is as close to wordless as possible. For a long time the idea that Gary Cooper might be an actor was thought a joke, and the same for Clark Gable, John Wayne, and their numerous heroic-type contemporaries who were "merely" personalities rather than actors. A Spencer Tracy, on the other hand, was certainly an actor because he could speak so well. This mistaken judgment was historically determined by the fact that movies were originally offshoots of the stage, and stage acting was something for which these heroes were indeed unfit. Their way of speaking was either silly and boyish, as in Wayne's case, whiny, as with Gable too much of the time, or monotonous, as with Cooper. But the point, which was missed because it was so new, was that all these heroes could show attitudes and feelings—usually simple and fundamental ones like anger or sexual desire, indignation or aggression—much better with their mouths shut than open. And even "show" is too strong a word—it is more accurate to say that they were eminently attributable actors. The mute human, like an animal, keeps all his possibilities intact, gives us nothing to make us doubt his reality, while any speech is bound to narrow his plausibility dangerously. Thus, there is a peculiar pressure on words in film to contribute to silent communication rather than monopolizing communication as words do on the stage. Words must above all be utilizable, each one as unadorned a story-mover as possible. The director's first instinct when faced with a multi-sentence speech is to pick it apart with a question for each word: "Why do we need this?" Needless to say, confronted with such a question, no Shakespeare play would last more than an hour.

When an actor talks he is more vulnerable to disbelief than when he is simply standing there. The very purpose of words in movies is to justify the silences that are the picture's main business. It is silence that creates an infinity of potential meaning that words can only diminish. This, I think, is also why very good prose writers do not usually prosper as screenwriters. Faulkner, Fitzgerald, Tennessee Williams, and a long line of eminent others discovered that their brightest stylistic inventions were precisely what movies reject like excrescences. Language tends to get in the way of the images, and the brighter the language, the more it draws attention to itself, the more it interferes.

The real poetry of a film lies first in its structure of

meaning, distinctly a function of the screenplay, and second in the expressiveness of its images, which are realized by the director but have their root if not more than that in the writer's work. Language, nevertheless, cannot be more than a servant to the images in the final impression.

Inevitably, especially if one is not accustomed to writing films, the question arises as to exactly why words are in such rivalry with the image as to be nearly self-indulgences. Even the wordy films that come to mind—Huston's *The Dead,* Capra's *Mr. Smith Goes to Washington,* Wilder's *Some Like It Hot* (a brilliantly and eminently *written* film by the late I. A. L. Diamond in collaboration with Wilder)—endure in memory not primarily for their lines but for the snap and marksmanship of their visual moods, their portraits of actors and settings, the things they have let us *see,* and the image-driven story. In the final analysis, dialogue exists at all in film in order to justify images and bridge them to sustain continuity. Dialogue is the musculature of the gestalt, the combination of images whose interactions create meaning. Altogether unlike the novel and even the play, film simply will not stand for writing that is basically commentary, however illuminating or beautiful or telling it may be. The closest one may safely verge on such adornment is in verbal wit, providing it is not convoluted, as it may be on the stage, but pithy and quickly understood. Otherwise, adornment and commentary are left to the director and his cinematographer, who indeed may elaborate through pleasurable explorations of things seen—locales, flesh, fingernails, eyes, all the wonders of the visible that film adores.

The reason or reasons for this image supremacy seem obvious: it is film's replication of dream, or more precisely, of our relationship to dreams. The film scene, even the apparently legato one, is always secretly in a hurry, much like its unacknowledged matrix, the dream scene, which flashes up in the sleeper and dies away in a matter of seconds. Dreams (if the reader's are anything like mine) are almost never verbal. Sometimes a single emblematic word, or perhaps two, may emerge in a dream scene as a clue (most likely ambiguous) to its intent, but everyone knows the dream in which people are avidly talking, with no words coming from their mouths, thus creating the image of talk rather than talk itself. We all know, too, the dream in which we are shouting a warning or a plea to others, with no sound issuing forth. Yet we know the meaning of what was being said or shouted. The meaning, in short, stems from the situation and not from the words we are trying to say about it. The dreamer is essentially deaf, and this suggests that film's origins, like those of dream, reach back to archaic stages of our evolution, to a period antedating our capacity to understand language, when we communicated in the primitive sign language of infancy. Long before he can understand words, the infant is obviously moved by what he sees, made frightened or happy or curious or anxious by purely visual stimuli. After a mere few months of life he has all the mental capacities required to direct movies or to paint pictures—everything, that is, except a grasp of the coherency of theme that brings relevance and meaning to what he is so pleasurably staring at.

For coherency's sake words—whether spoken or printed on the screen—are indeed necessary, however brief and minimal they may be, and this needs a screenwriter, someone capable of using words efficiently in order to make some sense of pleasure, or, to put it differently, in order to provide a social justification of sensuousness. But coherency in film remains distinctly secondary in importance to the enticing infantile riddle of sheer image itself.

The primitiveness of the image-story, growing as it does primarily from our very earliest months of life, tends to thin out the filmed tale in comparison to the word-driven one.

This is admittedly debatable and may be a purely personal reaction brought on by too many years in the theatre, but it seems to me the brain needn't work hard before a film; it can coast along in neutral. And perhaps this absence of effort simply makes one's appreciation that much shallower, for dreaming and movie watching are essentially passive activities, something happening *to* us, rather than an active and willful participation in another's imaginary world, as is the case with reading or even watching stage plays built on words instead of pictures.

Before a play we are forced to do the chores of editing, of deciding what is more or less important, of shifting our attention from actor to actor on the stage. In reading any text we have to decide and sometimes puzzle out what the words themselves mean. At the movies we decide nothing, our treasured infantile inertia is barely nudged, for the editor, the director, the lighting, the orchestration, and the overwhelming size of the image itself hand us an unmistakable hierarchy of importance and lay before us the predigested results to wonder at and enjoy. In point of fact, a film is even more primitive than a dream if we consider how far more densely packed with ambiguity and insoluble mystery dreams are. But it is their dream-born primitiveness that accounts for the universal attraction of movies, and it is perhaps the passivity with which they are viewed that supplies the delights of release and escape for people everywhere. A movie is something being done to us, and this is very nice relative to the other forms, which by comparison are work.

So the screenwriter, charged as he is with creating and maintaining coherency in the film, stands in some contradiction to its real nature and fundamental sources of pleasure, which are incoherent, subconscious, sensuous. Indeed, it has long been standard procedure to disinvite screenwriters from the sets and locations of the films they have written (although not this one). They are like a guilty conscience arriving at the scene of a crime, necessary for upholding civilization but not really much fun. Their presence crowds the director, inhibits the actors. In the usual orgy of creative play that filmmaking is, with actors and director and cinematographer seeking to fabricate real feelings and marvelous accidents, the screenwriter—who started it all—represents the principle of good order without which all meaning is likely to escape the enterprise. Naturally, he is suspect.

But he has one final satisfaction. He may, if he so desires, contemplate the amazing fact that from his typewriter clicking away in his lonely room veritable armies of people have sprung forth—actors, makeup artists, food concessionaires, explosives teams, horse wranglers, plane pilots, chauffeurs, bankers, ushers, box office people, ad men and women, sign painters, costumers, hair designers, frogmen, attending physicians, dentists, nurses, truck drivers, mechanics, turbine experts, electricians, and people who know how to stretch shoes quickly or disguise a sudden pimple, plus their spouses and lovers. And all these regiments from the same typewriter ribbon and a few score sheets of paper with words on them. Magic.

Without in the least belittling screenwriting, I would say that it does not require one to write very well. The often agonizing stylistic effort that writing normally demands is obviated, if only because the work is not written to be read. So in this sense screenwriting is easier than other forms. On the other hand, the human relationships, the thematic coherency, and the story in a *good* screenplay are as tough to get right as they are in any other form. I must add my own (probably minority) view, however, that the screenplay requires much more of a shorthand approach to scene writing than the stage play or the novel. It wants things indicated, and as deftly as possible, rather than fleshed out in words, perhaps because the actor's image on the screen is so vast and omnipotent as to be overwhelming in its suggestive power. What in other forms must be written out or spoken may on the screen be achieved with a raised eyebrow, the movement of a mouth or a hand, or a mere mute stare. But the condensation of image demanded by screenwriting is reminiscent of poetry as opposed to the prose of the stage form. In all, then, writing screenplays has its own formidable challenges, not the least of which is the capacity to bear the pleasure and the pain of being a member of the orchestra—in the first section, perhaps, but a member nonetheless—rather than playwright-soloist or novelist-virtuoso. The good part is that if the screenwriter gets less of the credit than he deserves, he may also get less of the blame, so it evens out in the end, and that, one supposes, is fair enough.

ARTHUR MILLER

CAST

ANGELA CRISPINI	Debra Winger
TOM O'TOOLE	Nick Nolte
JERRY	Will Patton
CONNIE	Judith Ivey
AMY	Kathleen Wilhoite
JUDGE HARRY MURDOCH	Jack Warden
CHARLEY HAGGERTY	Frank Converse
FELIX	Frank Military
FATHER MANCINI	Steven Skybell
JEAN	Mary Louise Wilson
BELLANCA	Mert Hatfield
SONNY	Peter Appel
MONTANA	Sean Weil
DEFENSE ATTORNEY	Timothy D. Wright
JUDGE	Elizabeth Ann Klein
REPORTER	James Parisi
DRIVER	R. M. Haley
JUDGE #2	T. M. Nelson George
STUNT COORDINATOR	David Ellis
UTILITY STUNT	Tim Davison
UTILITY STUNT	Don Pulford
UTILITY STUNT	Richard Allison

CREDITS

JEREMY THOMAS PRESENTS

A KAREL REISZ FILM

Nick Nolte   Debra Winger

Everybody Wins

Will Patton   Judith Ivey

and JACK WARDEN

Music by	Mark Isham
Additional Music by	Leon Redbone
Editor	John Bloom
Production Designer	Peter Larkin
Director of Photography	Ian Baker
Executive Producers	Linda Yellen
	Terry Glinwood
Co-produced by	Ezra Swerdlow
Screenplay by	Arthur Miller
Produced by	Jeremy Thomas
Directed by	Karel Reisz

© 1990 by Film Trustees Limited

Everybody Wins

Exterior: Highbury—Day

A car, several years old and never washed, is crossing a bridge linking countryside and a vista of a small New England town.

TOM O'TOOLE *is driving. Music is heard from his cassette-radio.*

We are introduced to Highbury—at least to its surface aspects—through the window of his moving car. It is a New England industrial city of perhaps forty thousand. While the white Colonial church may bespeak order and goodness, and some of the surrounding Victorian houses seem untouched by our century, there is an air of decay and uncertain development. The modern mall gives way to abandoned mills along the river, with smashed windows and storage areas covered by tall weeds. The firehouse, its gleaming machines within or being polished out front, is quickly overwhelmed by rickety slum areas with unemployed loungers on the streets.

Exterior: Angela's House—Day

We move into a nondescript working-class neighborhood and come to a stop before a house. TOM O'TOOLE *leaves the car and compares the house number with one he has jotted on a*

3

slip of paper. He rings the bell and waits, looking up and down the quiet street. He is in his forties, dressed in a small-town way, in a knee-length reversible.

He rings again, looking up at the windows, checks his watch, shakes his head in anger at himself as well as the absent person he's come to see, and starts back to his car in a beginning temper.

Exterior: Angela's House—Day

ANGELA, *high heels rapping, comes running up the street to him, already waving, wearing a low-cut dress and makeup too heavy for the morning, and carrying an incongruous attaché case in one hand, a fresh newspaper in the other. She is breathless.*

ANGELA: You're right on time! Hi!

TOM: Hi!

She holds out her hand, and he shakes it, somewhat thrown off.

ANGELA: You're even handsomer than on TV, aren't you? Sorry, but I had to run around and pick up my *New York Times.* They only get three a day in this town! (*She starts to the front door.*) Can we stop upstairs for a minute before we go to the penitentiary?

TOM: You misunderstood, Mrs. Crispini. I only agreed to *talk* today. I've got to know a lot more before I . . .

ANGELA: Oh, my God! . . . But I already told Felix you're coming! What happened? I sent you the transcript . . .

TOM (*discouraging*): I read the transcript.

ANGELA *mounts the stairs, continuing to talk and gesturing for him to follow—as he is obliged to do.*

Interior—Angela's House—Stairs—Day

ANGELA: But I told you on the phone, I've got other stuff you never *imagined.* I didn't sleep all night just thinkin' about him meetin' you today . . .

TOM: Well, I'm sorry if you misunderstood.

ANGELA (*at the apartment door*): Two minutes! Just to show you what I think of you . . . and not just lately!

Interior—Angela's Apartment—Day

They enter the room—a mess, an amazing profusion of bras, underwear, skirts, blouses, shoes. She has probably tried on her whole wardrobe and dropped it on the run before meeting him.

ANGELA: I can't tell you how thrilled—I mean, just for you to even be *considering* the case . . .

TOM: Well, I'm willing to listen.

ANGELA (*slipping a cassette into her VCR*): You remember this—a couple of months ago? The Baby Schmidlap case, the day you got the reversal?

On her TV screen, with the local courthouse in the background, a REPORTER *is talking into a mike, "breaking" a news story with the usual professional gusto.*

REPORTER: . . . The dramatic development came today when a new trial was ordered for Helen Schmidlap, who has been serving a ten-year prison term for the abduction of her own infant son . . .

ANGELA *pushes the fast-forward button. Cut to* TOM, *coming down the courthouse steps. The same* REPORTER *is waiting to speak to him.*

Here's Tom O'Toole, the investigator hired by the Schmidlap grandparents. Mr. O'Toole?

ANGELA *gives Tom's shoulder a little punch, pointing to his image on the screen.*

ANGELA: I mean, if that isn't *telegenic!*

On TV screen: The REPORTER *latches on to* TOM.

REPORTER: How do you feel about this victory, Mr. O'Toole?

TOM: Frankly, superb! The woman should never have been convicted in the first place!

TOM *moves off. The* REPORTER *turns to the camera.*

REPORTER: But State's Prosecutor Charles Haggerty this morning took issue with the decision . . .

On TV screen: Cut to HAGGERTY, *with courthouse in background.*

HAGGERTY *is a rather pompous, preppy type, but tough and intelligent and nattily dressed—about forty, nicely barbered, and not without humor. He is stepping forth to make a statement.*

ANGELA (*indicating* HAGGERTY *on TV screen*): You gotta admit he really carries a jacket.

HAGGERTY (*on TV screen*): I intend to try the defendant again, and you can be sure she will be convicted again, and of course the public will pay the cost again.

TOM (*to* ANGELA): What a clown!

HAGGERTY (*on TV screen*): I regret we have come to where so-called private investigators can shoot down the verdicts of faithful, hardworking juries and make a travesty of our whole system of justice!

ANGELA shuts off the machine.

TOM (*immensely excited and flattered*): What'd you tape that for?

ANGELA: Can I tell you in the car? Felix is really expecting us!

TOM opens his mouth to resist again, but his will has weakened before her insistence and the simple fact that she has opened the door and is standing there winsomely—and wittily—asking . . .

Please?

Exterior: Tom's Car—Day

TOM *and* ANGELA *are inside traveling through town.*

Interior: Tom's Car—Day

ANGELA: Can I call you Tom?

TOM: Sure.

ANGELA: Then you can stop calling me Mrs. Crispini.

He drives through town, heading for the Interstate. She takes out a cigarette, holds it for a moment, then returns it to the pack.

Anyway, I'm really a Finn. (*Slight pause.*) Which is not the same as a Swede. 'Cause you might hear people calling me "the Swede." (*Slight pause.*) Not that I was ever in Finland.

TOM *simply nods and grunts, glancing at her in fascination and puzzlement.*

I just can't believe I'm actually sitting next to you! I mean, to me, seeing you on TV fighting like that . . . (*She turns to him, confessionally.*) I might as well say it. To me, if there is such a thing as hope for the world, a man like you is it.

TOM (*with an embarrassed laugh*): Wish I could say the same. Tell me . . . what's your connection to this case?

ANGELA: In a few words? (*She is thoughtful for a moment, rapt, eagerly tense, trying to formulate a complicated thought. Then she gives up.*) We'll have to sit down. . . . I mean, it's very complicated. (*She draws a cigarette out and holds it, puts it between her lips, then returns it to the pack.*)

TOM: Don't you ever light them?

ANGELA: I'm bustin' my nuts trying to quit. So I go through the motions. Everything in the world is suggestion, you know—like one step away from a dream.

TOM (*mystified, yet drawn in*): It sure feels like it sometimes.

ANGELA: Like I had this doctor telling me I had cancer.

TOM *looks at her, concerned.*

But I don't.

TOM (*impressed*): How do you know?

ANGELA: Because. From the day I made up my mind, the pains stopped.

TOM: No kiddin'.

ANGELA: But of course I completely gave up alcohol. And sex.

TOM *gives her a doubtful look.*

You don't think it's possible?

TOM: Listen, the way you look I'd have to doubt it, but . . . I know it's *possible.*

ANGELA (*eyeing him with surprise*): Can I ask what you mean by that?

TOM: What I said.

ANGELA: But why sex?

TOM: I don't know. . . . The usual, I guess. Sooner or later Mother Nature can start to slow you down.

ANGELA: Really? At your age? And how do you feel without it? 'Cause it's purified me completely, I never felt . . . you know, this clean.

TOM: Well, that's good. I have sort of mixed feelings about it myself.

Interior: Penitentiary—Day

TOM, ANGELA, *and a* GUARD *walk down a corridor.*

Interior: Penitentiary Visitors' Room—Day

TOM *and* ANGELA *seat themselves in two adjoining chairs that face a long table dividing the room. The* GUARD *gives her a lusty glance and makes a super-appreciative gesture to*

TOM, *who seems a bit embarrassed but proud, too, of the implicit distinction. The* GUARD *leaves.*

ANGELA (*intimately*): It's so important you came. His appeal comes up on Thursday. We're claiming his lawyer was incompetent.

TOM: That's not very good grounds.

ANGELA (*searching in her attaché case*): Let me show you what he looked like when they arrested him. You're not going to believe this.

TOM (*probing*): Did you say you knew Felix before the murder?

ANGELA: Oh no, I never knew him till the trial. But Victor had been my doctor.

TOM: Victor? . . . Oh, you mean the man who was killed.

ANGELA: Dr. Victor Daniels. Didn't I mention that? He was a very wonderful friend to me.

TOM: Ah! Now I understand.

ANGELA: It got me so upset I couldn't sleep. I mean, to listen to that Haggerty going on day after day . . . and without evidence!

TOM: I may as well tell you—Charley Haggerty is the one reason I returned your call. That joker tried to get my license revoked, damn near put me out of business.

ANGELA (*realizing she has a newspaper clipping in her hand*): Oh! Here's Felix . . . before.

TOM *takes the clipping.*

Close-up: Photo of FELIX. *He is a conventional nineteen-*

year-old student with groomed flowing hair, open shirt, and zipper jacket.

Interior: Visitors' Room—Same Time

Close shot: FELIX *is shown in by a* GUARD. *He looks bewildered. He now has a head of straggly, tangled hair, a long beard, and haunted, frightened eyes. He stoops a bit. He seems a scared recluse living under a rock.*

ANGELA *immediately runs toward him, leaving* TOM *behind. She approaches* FELIX *delicately, unsure whether he recognizes her.*

ANGELA: Hello, dear. . . . It's Angela. You remember?

FELIX: You came back?

ANGELA: I always come back, dear!

ANGELA *takes his arm. The* GUARD *makes a move to stop her, but she gives him a sweet, helpless look that disarms him.*

Interior: Visitors' Room—Later

TOM, ANGELA, *and* FELIX *have been sitting here for some time.* TOM *is leafing through the transcript. He speaks without looking up.*

TOM: I'm trying to get a feel for this case. Maybe I can come up with some angle for Mrs. Crispini to run down.

ANGELA: You don't look like you're eating, Felix.

FELIX: They cook everything in antiseptic.

ANGELA: But you have to eat.

TOM (*taking charge*): You live in Boston, Felix—how do you

come to be down in Highbury the night your uncle was killed?

FELIX: I had a date.

TOM: With your uncle?

ANGELA (*to* FELIX, *sympathetically*): Can I tell him? (*To* TOM:) He knows this girl Cindy here in Highbury. They had a date, but she didn't show. (*She gives* TOM *a "See, he's a helpless kid" look.*) Mr. O'Toole can help you, Felix. Why'd you go see your uncle?

FELIX: 'Cause I was down there anyway. My mom was always on me to go see Uncle Victor. She thought he could get me into pharmacy school.

TOM: Pharmacy school?

FELIX: Yeah, he was a doctor. He knew all the people on the boards.

ANGELA: That was Victor—always ready to help people.

TOM (*considers the transcript and nods, understanding*): What was the first notification you had of your uncle's murder, Felix?

FELIX: I read it in the paper. I nearly fainted—cut up like a chicken in his living room.

TOM: And what next?

FELIX: These two Boston detectives come around—"Can we look at your comb, sir?" "Sure"—I give it to them. Next day, I'm under arrest.

TOM (*nods again, still leafing through the transcript*): There's no mention of your friend Cindy in the transcript.

FELIX (*suddenly crying out*): Because my lawyer couldn't be bothered to call her in! They'd break for lunch, he'd go read a poetry book! That man destroyed me. And for that he charged twenty-five thousand dollars, my mother's last penny!

ANGELA: Ssh! Everything's going to change now, dear. (*She massages Felix's shoulders.*)

FELIX: Look, I got to tell you . . . this lady has been really good to me. But . . . I'm not here anymore. I mean I'm walking around, but I'm dead. (*He weeps softly.*)

TOM (*resisting sentiment*): I'll be quick. Felix, I'd like you to listen—Felix?

ANGELA: Listen to him, dear.

TOM: In the house that night . . . can you remember? Did you comb your hair?

FELIX: You mean in front of my uncle?

TOM: How about in the bathroom?

FELIX: But they found the tooth of my comb in the living room—and right next to the body, for God's sake.

TOM: Not in their first report. Only days later, on a second search.

FELIX: You mean it was moved there?

TOM (*shrugging*): Possible.

Interior—Penitentiary Corridor—Day

The GUARD *is leading* TOM *and* ANGELA *out. She has a*

remarkably intense look on her face. She seems elevated, and at the same time somehow sensually charged up.

ANGELA: My God! Your face. . . . You suddenly looked like the sun shooting out lights.

TOM (*bewildered, but flattered*): What?

The GUARD *looks on doubtfully.*

ANGELA (*taking Tom's arm*): Oh, Tom . . . you've got to take this case. You were born for this!

TOM (*warily, yet drawn by her strange intensity*): Let me think about it. I don't know. Maybe I can look in on the hearing. I frankly don't know what to tell you.

Exterior: Highbury Courthouse—Day

TOM, *checking his watch, makes his way up the courthouse steps.*

Interior: Courtroom—Day

The scene is from Tom's point of view. He is seated at the back of the courtroom, observing as the DEFENSE ATTORNEY *concludes his appeal to the bench while Prosecutor* HAGGERTY *awaits his turn. Chief of Detectives* BELLANCA *looks on, seated at Haggerty's side.*

ANGELA *sits in another part of the room, attaché case on her lap, pad and pencil at the ready.*

DEFENSE ATTORNEY: It comes down, Your Honor, to the perfectly obvious fact that the defendant Felix Daniels did not have competent counsel. He failed to bring up important evidence which I have presented to the court today.

For this and other reasons we appeal to the court for a new trial.

JUDGE: Mr. Haggerty?

HAGGERTY: Your Honor, defendant's counsel was very successful in numerous other cases. He is a well-known attorney with a reputable law firm. Felix Daniels was convicted of a bloody and brutal murder. There is not the slightest doubt about his guilt.

> ANGELA *violently shakes her head: "No!"*

. . . The evidence is damning and complete. This appeal has absolutely no basis in fact. The State asks that it be denied.

> TOM *observes that* HAGGERTY *has shot a glance toward* ANGELA, *but its meaning is not clear to him. Does he know her, or is it simply that he has suddenly noticed a strange woman in the empty courtroom?*

JUDGE: Defendant's appeal for a new trial is denied.

> *Interior: Courthouse Corridor—Day*
>
> TOM *and* ANGELA *are about to turn a corner in the corridor when they nearly run into* HAGGERTY, *who sets his face in a wide grin. He seems not to have noticed* ANGELA *at all and keeps moving.*

HAGGERTY: O'Toole! What brings you here! I haven't seen any cameras.

TOM (*holds up a finger with a wry grin*): Wait!

> *They are both angrily intense and pretend to laugh. As they*

pass each other, ANGELA *throws* HAGGERTY *a private, impenetrable look. He responds with a blank stare and walks on.*

Exterior: Judge Murdoch's Office Building—Day

ANGELA, *preoccupied, is getting into Tom's car, which is parked in front of an office building near the courthouse. A chauffeur-driven car draws into a reserved space nearby. Judge* HARRY MURDOCH *emerges just in time to catch a glimpse of* ANGELA *disappearing into Tom's car. Meanwhile, the judge's secretary,* JEAN, *a middle-aged woman, gets out of his car with his papers and briefcase, and waves to* TOM *like a friend.*

MURDOCH: Tom!

TOM: Judge! I been meaning to call you.

MURDOCH (*ribbing him about* ANGELA): Not bad! What's that?

TOM: Terrific woman . . .

MURDOCH (*teasingly*): Client?

TOM (*shrugs, pretending it's all routine*): I dunno. She's got a wild story. . . . This Felix Daniels who was sent away for slicing up his uncle? She claims she's got proof he didn't do it.

MURDOCH (*not very interested*): That so? Just don't forget, kid—most of the people in jail belong there. (*He moves away.*) Come by the house when you have a minute. We'll play some pool. (*He goes into his office building.*)

Exterior: Angela's Block—Day

Tom's car pulls up in front of the house.

Interior: Tom's Car—Same Time

ANGELA *is opening the passenger door. She lingers.*

ANGELA: I'm scared. I don't know what Felix will do now that the appeal's lost. Incidentally, his mother has a business. She could give you like maybe five hundred down . . .

TOM: That'd be nice. And what's in it for you?

ANGELA (*genuinely surprised*): Me!

TOM: I'm sorry, kid, but I still don't understand your connection.

ANGELA: Come up, will you? (*With a mixture of seductiveness and some unexplained anxiety she grips his arm, smiling wittily.*) I get so little chance to talk to anyone who isn't stepping on his own fingers. I mean, Christ, you look like a *man!*

TOM (*laughs, flattered*): Hey, gimme a break, will ya?

ANGELA: Please!

TOM: So what's your idea? Who would want to frame Felix?

ANGELA: They're watching.

TOM (*his aggressive juices flowing as he glances at the street*): Who's watching?

ANGELA: On the corner. Cops.

He turns to look up the street, then in the other direction.

They just pulled out.

Her fear is so palpable that as she gets out of the car he gets out too, and they head for her door.

TOM: You sure? I didn't see anybody.

With a trembling hand, ANGELA *works her key nervously in the lock. He helps insert the key.*

Interior: Angela's Apartment—Moments Later

The living room is practically bare, with no personality, as if the room is never used.

ANGELA: Lock the door, will ya?

TOM *does, with a lock and a safety chain.* ANGELA *calls from the bedroom.*

Come on in.

Interior: Angela's Bedroom—Same Time

TOM *enters the bedroom. This time he has a moment to examine it. It is a crowded, intensely lived-in, cavelike room. He observes* ANGELA *neatening up, scooping up the debris of underwear, bras, stockings, skirts, blouses, shoes, scattered everywhere.*

ANGELA: Be with you in a second. . . . Would you like some vitamins?

TOM: Use your phone?

ANGELA: Sure! (*She swings the door of the bathroom open and goes in, closing it behind her.*)

TOM (*picks up the phone beside her bed and dials*): Me, Connie. Any calls? . . . Thanks, I'll see him tomorrow. . . . Well, it sounds like another Charley Haggerty special. . . . Yeah, he was the prosecutor. But I don't think I want to get into it. Thanks.

He hangs up and looks around the room—the rumpled bed

*covered with a satin throw, the worn carpet, the plastic-tufted
headboard. Finally he spots a surprising shelf of books and
walks over to inspect the titles. Under it is a drape, partly
open, revealing a four-drawer filing cabinet once he gently
moves it aside. A heavy padlock has been affixed to the
drawers. He lets the drape fall closed again.*

ANGELA (*off screen*): Are you working on a case?

TOM (*disparagingly*): Just routine stuff. I work for insurance
companies now and then, pick up some easy money.

ANGELA (*off screen*): That must be very interesting.

TOM: Molto boring. I run checks on new executives. This
one's gonna be made vice-president of a ball-bearin' company, and they want to know if he's gay.

ANGELA (*off screen*): Jeeze, they still doin' that?

TOM: Well, you can't have a homosexual vice-president of a
ball-bearin' company. (*He picks up the transcript. He wants to
get on with things.*)

ANGELA (*entering*): Well! This is better! (*She is in a very nearly
transparent negligee, which forces him instinctively to glance
down and away.*)

TOM (*almost sniggering*): Boy, that's quite a little outfit there.

ANGELA (*stretching out on the bed*): Like some herb tea?

TOM: No, I'm fine. Now listen . . . I've got an hour's drive
home.

> ANGELA *sits up on the bed. As much to ward off her invita-
> tion as anything else, he sits on the edge of a chair looking
> very businesslike.*

ANGELA: There's a lot bigger case here than meets the eye, Tom.

TOM (*equivocally*): Maybe you better not tell me.

ANGELA: I guess so, if you're staying out of it. But you're breaking my heart, y'know.

TOM: Tell you the truth, it's got that old familiar stink, but I don't see myself locking horns with the system again.

ANGELA: The man who does this case is going to need a pair of brass balls. Which I happen to think is what you've got.

TOM (*flattered*): I know, but the time comes when you realize the public has to love the corruption or you wouldn't have all these crooked judges falling out of the trees every ten minutes, and they wouldn't be electing the likes of Charley Haggerty to run the criminal justice system.

ANGELA: You're a thrill just to listen to. I mean, you can talk about something else besides money and pussy.

TOM: Yeah, well . . . (*He is holding the transcript in his hand, preparing to leave.*) Let me mull it over in my mind some more. . . . It was great meeting you.

ANGELA: I know the murderer.

TOM (*stopped cold, but trying to remain cool and skeptical*): Yeah?

The issue is her credibility, and she stares him right in the eye.

That raises a number of questions, doesn't it?

ANGELA: Oh, the cops know him too. In fact, they had him.

TOM: And?

ANGELA: They let him go.

TOM: Why?

ANGELA: That is the story.

TOM: Would you be ready to talk about this?

ANGELA: I am ready. But there's still a couple of things I need to prove. That's why I need you. Felix is the tip of the iceberg. . . . God. I'm exhausted. (*She pats the mattress as she stretches out on the bed.*) Could you sit a minute before you go?

He sits beside her on the bed.

You mind if I touch your hand?

TOM: Don't try to crank me up, kid.

ANGELA: I talk better when I'm touching. According to the paper . . . you got priests in the family?

TOM: A brother. But it never rubbed off on me.

ANGELA: I'm more into it since my cancer scare. I have a friend, Father Mancini at Saint Jude's?

TOM: Don't know him.

Her sensuous openness to him is becoming unabashed. He sees it plainly and is aroused.

ANGELA: When I told him my feelings about you—the kind of fighter you are—he said, "God places certain people on this earth to fight for truth and justice." He thinks you're one. And I'm another. You mind if I kiss you? (*Before he can react she is drawing him down and kissing him, rather chastely, temptingly.*) You could wrap up the case in a month. I know what to look for and where to look.

Her hand moves down his body. He is exploding with surprise.

Hey! What's this about Mother Nature lettin' you down!

He is on her before his brain can begin to catch up.

Exterior: Tom's House—Evening

TOM *has a comfortable, conventional ranch house out in the country; the nearest neighbor is a faraway light. Tom's car coming up the road to the house sets off the delighted yelping of his dog, who races up to the car as Tom pulls in beside a five-year-old Volvo. Lights are on in the house.*

TOM *gets out of the car in great spirits. His Labrador runs up to him, waving his tail.* TOM *plays with him, roughhousing in the fading light.*

Through the window we see CONNIE, *his sister, working at papers on the dining room table. She reacts to Tom's arrival only by lifting her head, and he takes her presence for granted.*

Interior: Tom's Dining Room, Kitchen, "Office"—Night

The pleasant house has an open kitchen to one side, separated from the dining area by a bar. On the other side is an alcove with an office desk, steel files, typewriter and phone, a couple of office chairs, and a swivel chair.

CONNIE *is correcting exam papers at the dining room table. She is in her mid-forties, a nervous smoker with a brittle humor, intelligent and determined to carry on no matter what.*

TOM *takes a burger out of the microwave and flops it onto a plate. He grabs the ketchup bottle and shakes it over the burger. It's empty.*

TOM: Out of ketchup, Connie. (*He brings the burger and utensils to the table.*)

CONNIE: This was your day for shopping. You told me to pressure you, so I'm pressuring you.

TOM: Right. Well, keep it up. (*He wolfs his food while glancing over some of the scattered papers. He picks one up and points to a word.*) What's this word supposed to be?

CONNIE: "Apparently."

TOM (*spelling*): A-p-o-r-o-n-d-l-y? And you're giving him a B?

CONNIE: He's captain of the swimming team.

TOM (*with a big nod*): Boy, that's real creative spelling.

CONNIE: I don't dare flunk him, there'd be a riot. . . . I can't remember anymore—was everything always so corrupt?

   The phone rings.

TOM (*briefly caressing her face*): You're too pure, Connie.

   TOM *gets up and goes around the bar to his office area. As he picks up the phone, we see the photos on his desk: an eight-by-ten photo of Tom and Catherine, his late wife; nearby, a photo of his parents, the father in a policeman's uniform; a younger man, a brother, in clerical garb; and high school graduation photos of two teenage sons.* TOM *speaks into the phone.*

Ya? Oh, hi!

ANGELA (*voice-over, through phone*): Could you come over right away?

TOM (*checking his watch*): Now? It's almost midnight.

CONNIE *looks up, curious, amused.*

ANGELA (*voice-over*): I'm missing you very bad. . . . You were wonderful.

TOM: Well, I'm glad you feel that way . . .

CONNIE *lights another cigarette and pretends to go back to her grading.*

ANGELA (*voice-over*): Tom? (*Pause.*) You with somebody?

TOM (*privately*): My sister.

ANGELA (*voice-over*): Oh! . . . You're not married?

TOM: My wife passed away three years ago. Look, I'll go see that girl for you tomorrow.

ANGELA (*voice-over*): Great! Can we have dinner after?

TOM: Sure.

ANGELA (*voice-over*): Good night. I'm really grateful.

TOM *hangs up, flushed. He comes back to the table.* CONNIE *gives him a brief glance, noticing his tension, then looks at her papers.* TOM *attacks the cold hamburger.*

CONNIE: Could I say something? Unless you'd rather I didn't.

TOM: What?

CONNIE (*indicating phone*): This Crispini woman . . . she sounds absolutely ditzy to me.

TOM: I would prefer librarians, but they rarely know where the bodies are buried.

CONNIE: But you don't really know who she is, what her

connection is to the case. Isn't there something strange about that?

TOM (*both uncomfortable and relieved to bypass the sexual issue*): Look, I'm not committed, but I can't just walk away. She says she knows who killed that doctor.

CONNIE: Then why doesn't she just come out and tell you who it is?

TOM (*defensively, because she's making sense*): The woman's scared. It's understandable.

CONNIE (*laughs nervously, trying to affect amusement*): She really got you going, didn't she!

TOM (*blushing, and on the verge of resentment*): What do you mean, got me going?

CONNIE: Sssh! Please, I'm sorry. It's none of my business . . . (*She picks up her cup and starts to the kitchen, relieved to change the subject.*) Listen, the school got a block of tickets for *Rigoletto* in Boston next week. Should I get a couple? We could drive up and have lobster and . . .

TOM: Hey, I'd love that! But let me let you know tomorrow, all right?

CONNIE (*sighs, grinning*): Okay . . . no *Rigoletto*.

Exterior: Outskirts of Highbury—Cemetery—Day

Tom's car is proceeding slowly on a disused, narrow side road that skirts a cemetery. He stops and gets out.

Tom's point of view: A fire is burning among the gravestones. Two men, BIKERS in leather jackets, can be seen indistinctly through the smoke, tending the fire or tending a grave. Their elaborate, shining motorcycles are parked nearby.

Exterior: Outskirts of Highbury—Amy's House—Day

Walking on, TOM *notices a dirt driveway leading to a small, gloomy house surrounded by trees and wild brush. He starts walking down this driveway. A rifle shot. He halts. A second shot. He steps behind a tree and watches.*

Tom's point of view: In front of the house is AMY, *a stringy young woman wearing jeans, a bandanna, and a man's coat. She is just lowering a shotgun, which is pointed off-screen, not at* TOM.

TOM *steps out from behind the tree.*

TOM: Excuse me . . .

AMY *screams in shock and almost drops the shotgun, paralyzed. He approaches her. She is drug-pale.*

Sorry about that.

AMY: There's a woodchuck. He's always . . . like, comin' around.

TOM: No kiddin'. I guess you must be Amy, right?

AMY: Why? . . .

TOM: I'm Mr. O'Toole. Angela talked to you this morning on the phone. Said I was coming.

AMY *simply waits, expectantly.*

I'm not the police. I'm a private investigator. I'm looking into the Dr. Daniels murder.

A phone rings in the distance, in the house. Clutching the shotgun, AMY *runs to the house and goes in.*

The sound of motorbikes makes him turn. The two BIKERS *from the cemetery ride past the house and recede into the distance.*

Interior: Amy's House—Same Time

TOM *cautiously opens the screen door. A frightened chicken flies out past his head.*

Amy's living room is a mess: broken couch, half a dozen chickens strolling around, a general air of drug-ridden decay. On one of the walls is a poster featuring the famous image from Vietnam days of the monk's sacrifice by fire. A crude picture of St. Sebastian is propped on a decaying mantelpiece.

AMY *sits slumped in a chair, the shotgun across her knees.*

AMY (*gesturing vaguely toward the telephone*): It's for you . . .

TOM *crosses to the phone, where the receiver lies off the hook. He doesn't take his eyes off* AMY *and the gun. He picks up the phone.*

TOM (*into the phone*): Hello?

ANGELA (*voice-over, through phone*): I changed my mind. I don't want you talking to Amy without I'm there. Meet me for dinner and I'll explain, okay?

She hangs up. TOM *is puzzled. He hangs up.* AMY *sits there, staring at nothing.* TOM *reaches down into an upturned hat and pulls out . . . an egg!*

AMY: That's an egg.

TOM (*congratulates her, as though at least this is some progress*):
Right!

AMY: Jerry doesn't live here anymore.

TOM (*gently replacing the egg*): Which Jerry is that?

AMY: The one that killed that Dr. Daniels . . .

TOM (*waits a beat, straight-faced*): I wonder if you could help
me out, Amy. See, I'm comin' in a little late. . . . You know,
don't you, that there's a man in prison for killing Dr.
Daniels.

AMY: Oh no, he didn't do it. Jerry did it.

TOM: Gee whiz, that's what Angela's been tellin' me. Incidentally, I guess you and her are old friends, huh?

AMY: Angela? . . . Yeah, from Bimini.

TOM: Bimini? . . . You mean down the Caribbean?

AMY (*with a changed expression, seeming to relate momentarily*): I
told all this to the cops, though. . . . And then Jerry went
down.

TOM: Jerry went where, dear?

AMY: To the cops. He was all covered with blood.

TOM: And what did the cops do?

AMY: They sent him right back here to go to sleep.

TOM: He told the cops he'd killed Dr. Daniels?

AMY: He was going crazy about it, so I said, "You better get it
off your mind"—'cause he's so religious. He's raised Catholic, you know.

TOM: You wouldn't know where I could find Jerry now, would you?

AMY: He might be in the cemetery, but he's not dead.

TOM: What's he doing in the cemetery if he's not dead, dear?

> *Sleep threatens to overcome* AMY. *She slips deeper into the chair.*

Amy?

AMY: Well, praying there to Major McCall.

TOM (*totally flummoxed, therefore totally cool*): Praying to Major McCall?

AMY: Or else he's at the mill . . . (*She breathes deeply and falls fast asleep.*)

> *Exterior: Cemetery—Dusk*
>
> *Camera holds on the plinth of a monument. The monument itself has been removed. Tom's hand touches broken cement that once joined the two. Smoke from the dying fire nearby makes him cough.*

TOM *inspects the scene. He reads the inscription. Close up:*

> MAJOR JEROME SETH MCCALL
> POET AND SOLDIER
> HIS LIFE FOR THE NATION
> *1825–1862*

TOM *stoops to look at the fire. Among the embers he can make out the remnants of what looks like a little pile of animal bones. The grass around is blackened. He stands and walks toward his car.*

Exterior: Tom's Car—Dusk

TOM *is driving along a road above the river when he sees:*

Exterior: Abandoned Mill—Dusk

Tom's point of view: Beside the river is a large, long-abandoned New England mill. Far away and indistinctly, he sees a courtyard—a shambles, with a profusion of broken machinery, motorbikes, tractors. A crudely painted sign—"Jerry's"—hangs over an entrance.

Closer shot: TOM *leaves his car and approaches the mill, which appears deserted. After a moment he hears the roar of motorbikes. One, two, three* BIKERS *emerge from the mill and roar past him, almost knocking him down. Then a fourth biker speeds past, and* TOM *sees the name "Jerry" spelled out in chrome studs.*

TOM, *now alone, moves into the mill.*

Interior: The Mill—Workshop—Dusk

A large space has been turned into a workshop for motorcycles and other machinery. Workbenches and tools are scattered about, and the lights are still on. A coffee urn hisses and drips in a corner.

TOM *walks through the workshop. It's been so recently vacated that he wonders if somebody's still there. A kerosene stove with a pot on it, a few cans of beans. At the far end of the workshop a set of swinging doors made of plastic.*

Interior: The Mill—The "Tabernacle"—Dusk

TOM *comes into another large space. The light from the windows is sepulchral. As his eyes adjust, he sees an object standing against a wall, a statue of a Civil War major, sword in scabbard, proudly moustachioed, one foot forward—the conventional Civil War monument. It has been placed on a rough base, a wooden crate. A few candles stand before it.*

Now he sees a live lamb in a makeshift pen.

He walks to a wide loading door on the water side of the building and looks out on a landing ramp or pier.

He turns now to go back to the workshop—and practically walks into ANGELA.

TOM: Jesus! . . . Boy, you scared me! Whatcha doin' here?

She stares at him strangely, without immediately answering. Her eyes seem to see inward rather than out. Trying to make contact, he grins, noting the burning cigarette in her mouth.

You back smoking again?

She gives him a mystified look, as though she doesn't know what he's referring to. She carries herself differently than before—with a certain aloof elegance, her vocal tones deeper in the throat and cultivated, although the grammar is not quite perfect.

ANGELA: I thought we agreed that you weren't coming here.

TOM (*mystified, searching her odd look*): Well, Amy said Jerry might be here . . .

ANGELA: What "Amy said" is hardly consequential.

TOM (*absolutely baffled*): Hey, look, I'm only . . .

ANGELA (*with haughty command*): We're going to have to discuss this if you intend to continue.

TOM (*decides to let this pass and points to the Major's statue and the penned lamb*): What's this about, do you know?

ANGELA (*glancing down at the sacrifice, with a loaded quality to her simple reply*): It's his religion.

TOM: Jerry?

She looks up at the Civil War statue, and it seems to touch her with some reverential feeling, which she instantly dispels.

ANGELA (*factually*): He believes the Major is God and that he's his son.

As she speaks, TOM detects the barest suggestion that she may share this belief and is feeling out his reaction.

TOM: Well, he's got a right, I guess. Is this a one-man religion or . . .

ANGELA: Oh, there's a group. Our father's house has many mansions, you know.

TOM *doesn't reply, trying to fathom her.*

I want you to tell me before you decide to take off after somebody. You could get hurt, you understand?

TOM: Look, if I'm doing the investigation, I make those decisions, not you, Angela.

ANGELA (*turns to walk away*): Why are you calling me that kind of name?

TOM: Hey, hold it! What name you want me to call you?

ANGELA (*flaring up*): Why, Renata, of course. Don't you understand *anything*?

TOM (*pauses, then speaks in a friendly but decisive tone*): You want to tell me what's going down here?

She ignores him.

Or should I go home and stay there?

ANGELA (*walking away*): I must say, your insensitivity comes
as rather a surprise.

TOM: What is all this elocution all of a sudden?

ANGELA: I'm speaking English. I'm terribly sorry if you find
that confusing!

And she is off. TOM *watches her, bewildered, as she clip-clops
away through the debris of the yard.*

Fade-out.

Fade-in:

Exterior: Tom's House—Early Morning

In the morning light we see TOM *looking out the window with
a pair of binoculars. He is at his desk talking on the phone, but
we can't hear what he's saying.*

Interior: Tom's House—Same Time

As TOM *looks through the binoculars, he's conducting a
business conversation on the phone. His manner is relaxed but
uninvolved.*

TOM (*into phone*): Tell you what. Let me do a background
check, and you can decide if you want surveillance as a
follow-up. . . . Now, who'd you like me to bill this to? The
company? . . . Fine. . . . About a week from now.

Exterior: Tom's House—Bird Feeder—Same Time

Cutaway to what TOM *is watching: a tall bird feeder sus-*

pended from the bare branch of a tree a little distance from the house. Wild birds flock to the feeder.

Interior: Tom's House—Same Time

TOM *is at his desk, papers spread out for work, cup of coffee at his elbow.* CONNIE *sits nearby, reading.*

TOM (*finishing phone conversation*): I'll send you both copies. . . . Yeah, thanks for calling. (*He hangs up. To* CON-NIE:) I thought that was a cardinal for a second.

CONNIE (*comes to look out the window*): No . . . just a robin.

TOM *puts down the binoculars. The transcript of Felix's trial is lying on his desk, open to the section of photographs.*

Insert: Trial photograph showing the hideously mangled body of Dr. Daniels, bloody and decapitated. A label reads, "Exhibit 21."

TOM: Incidentally, I've just about decided to cut out of that Daniels case.

CONNIE: Boy, that's good news.

TOM: Well, some of her information checked out, but . . . she's just too complicated.

CONNIE: I thought she sounded off the wall from day one.

TOM: It's like chasing feathers in a tornado. I'm telling her this afternoon.

Close-up: TOM, *conflicted. As he tries to stay with this resolve, his gaze falls on the transcript again.*

Exterior: Bridge into Highbury—Day

Tom's car is crossing the bridge. Restless, he is listening to one of his tapes.

Exterior: Angela's House—Day

Tom's car is parked outside Angela's house. After a moment, he comes out. He looks up and down the street to see if ANGELA *might by chance be coming home.*

He gets back into the car. Just before driving off he checks the rearview mirror in which he first saw ANGELA *appear a couple of weeks ago. No luck this time. He drives off.*

Exterior: Highbury Street—Afternoon

TOM *walks along, his eye is caught by photos of women on magazine covers at a newsstand; he walks on and can't help noticing a woman's leg as she steps into a bus; a lingerie shop window attracts his eye. He goes into a coffee shop.*

Interior: Coffee Shop—Afternoon

TOM *sits at the counter and opens the trial transcript, turning pages. The waitress halts before him.*

TOM: Coffee, please.

He notices a woman seated at a nearby table. She is folding one leg over another, and it seems to catch his heart. He sips his coffee, turning transcript pages, until he comes to a photograph and holds it down to study it.

Insert: Photo of Daniels' million-dollar home. Under it a label reads, "Exhibit 3—House of Dr. Victor Daniels."

Exterior: Daniels' House—Day

We see the same house in reality, except now it is overgrown with weeds and boarded up. Some second-floor windows are broken. There is a deserted dog kennel by the side.

TOM *is looking at the house. He works his way to a boarded window.*

Interior: Daniels' House—Day

The interior is dark. Slits of daylight fall through the boarded-up windows. TOM, *outside, rips away a couple of boards and climbs in. He turns on a flashlight with a powerful beam and begins to move through the house, which has been emptied—appliances ripped out, fixtures torn away. Broken glass, empty beer bottles, and cigarette butts litter the floor, suggesting previous intruders. There are graffiti and not quite legible initials on the walls as the flashlight moves past.*

Tom's light finds the police outline of Daniels' body on the floor—to which vandals have added eyes, a penis, a hat. He moves the light up the wall. A circle is crudely painted around a stain with an arrow pointing to it and "Doc's brains" scrawled alongside. High on the wall, above a huge splash of bloodstains, he sees more graffiti: "Love ya Jerry!"

TOM *stands still in the midst of this ruin, trying to absorb some message from its silence.*

Exterior: Bar—Night

TOM *is seen from the street, seated at a table by the window, staring intently, lost at the edge of the mystery.*

Interior: Bar—Night

It is the dead hour. There are perhaps six people in the bar, two or three drinking in the background, a couple eating at a table, two men watching hockey on TV. The BARTENDER *is leaning back, arms folded, staring out the window at the street.* TOM *has not moved; he sits before an untouched grinder sandwich and a full glass of beer whose head has evaporated.*

Now the BARTENDER *glances over at* TOM, *curious at his isolation.*

Closer shot: TOM *is concentrating on what he saw at Daniels' house, his thoughts far away from his surroundings: where to begin to solve this thing, how to even start?*

The BARTENDER *glances at him again, his curiosity piqued by Tom's obliviousness and his not touching his food or beer.*

TOM *now stands and starts for the door. The* BARTENDER, *surprised, starts to react.* TOM *stops, puts his hand in his pocket, and lays a bill on the bar.*

TOM: Sorry. (*He exits.*)

Exterior: Bar—Night

TOM *is coming out of the restaurant, vaguely surveying the street before him. Where to look? How to begin?*

Exterior: Main Street—Cinema—Night

The moviehouse displays a sexy poster. Main Street is nearly deserted. The show over, a group of loud TEENAGERS *emerges, then a trickle of* MIDDLE-AGED CUSTOMERS, *among them* TOM. *He gets to the street, looks up and down, restless, doesn't quite know which way to go. As the teenagers disperse on motorbikes,* TOM *wanders past the empty shops. He notices a woman alone on the street.*

He stops in front of a boutique window that shows forms in negligees, bras, upturned legs in pantyhose. It is a corner window. Looking through it, he sees the lone figure on the other side of the street—a woman wearing sunglasses. She is like a chimera at first. For a moment he only senses her identity instinctually, but she pauses before a shop window, and the light on her shows she is ANGELA.

Some instinct restrains him from going to her immediately. He watches her instead as she moves along waywardly, clearly with no destination. An unhappy loneliness seems to grip her. He follows at a distance.

A big car pulls up beside her, and the DRIVER—*unheard by* TOM—*propositions her. She stands there, not trying to escape, as though she might be considering his deal. The* DRIVER *opens his door and gets out. Tom's face shows his near-anger, his jealousy.*

But now she turns and walks away. The DRIVER *is furious, yells after her.*

DRIVER: All right—a hundred!

She doesn't turn back.

Ah, go f— (*He gets back in his car and drives off.*)

ANGELA *moves on down the street, again without purpose, glancing at shop windows or halting to look up at the sky.* TOM *sees her take out a cigarette, light it, and inhale. Is she expecting to meet someone, or is she simply lost?*

He makes the decision and walks to overtake her. A few yards behind her he calls out.

TOM: Ange, . . . hey! Angela!

She doesn't turn around. Now he is a few feet behind her.

Renata?

ANGELA (*turns now, immensely happy to see him*): Hello! Where you been, why haven't you called me?

TOM: Listen, what am I supposed to call you, Renata or Angela? (*He sees her look of amnesiac confusion descending.*)

ANGELA: Renata?

TOM: You know . . . over Jerry's place, when you laid me out with all those adjectives . . .

ANGELA: Oh, God. Did I do a number or something?

She breaks off, the blood draining out of her face. He grips her arm, mystified. Her finger is burned by the end of her ciga-rette, which she seems shocked to find herself holding. She flings it down and looks at it as if it were some alien thing.

Get me home, will you?

Alarmed, TOM helps her to walk, but as they start off, a car slows in front of them. BELLANCA, seated beside the DRIVER, simply looks at her as the car moves away.

TOM *sees her turn away from Bellanca's look, with what seems not only fear but something like shame. They move off, his arm supporting hers.*

Exterior: Tom's Car—Outside a Roadside Diner—Night

TOM *and* ANGELA *are inside the car talking. There is a lot of activity around them from boisterous teenagers and bikers. The lights from passing cars keep playing across their faces.*

ANGELA *is deeply upset, staring ahead. There has clearly been a break in their talk, an impasse of some kind.*

TOM: You're not listening to me. All I'm saying is that I'm not really gettin' the story from you, which I respect because it's your business, but I gotta face it, I can't work in the dark. So I'm thinking seriously of pullin' out of this. . . . I mean . . .

He breaks off as she turns to him, her look incredulous, deeply shocked and lost. And his resolve begins to weaken as he realizes her need.

ANGELA: Okay, Tom. (*She gives his arm a pat.*) I know when I lose. But I'm not giving up on Felix. (*She removes her glasses.*)

TOM (*seeing a bruise*): What happened to your eye?

ANGELA (*with a wave of disgust*): Oh, it doesn't matter. (*She starts to open the car door.*)

TOM (*suddenly takes her hand, his look desperate*): See, my problem is I don't think I want to lose you.

ANGELA (*with a sad but witty grin and a toss of her head*): Then don't.

TOM (*delaying the end*): Honey, if you would only open up with me! 'Cause I'd really, *really* love to put the fear of God in that college-boy prosecutor and shake him out of the tree just to see what drops out with him, you know?

ANGELA: Do I love brass balls! (*She grasps his face and plants a deep kiss on his mouth.*)

TOM: I love you, Angela. (*He quickly grips his head.*) Now what the hell'd I say that for!

ANGELA: Oh, you're dear!

Interior: Angela's House—Night

Angela's room is in more than usual disarray. Besides her own scatter of clothes we see Tom's, discarded after lovemaking. TOM and ANGELA lie side by side, his arm protectively around her. Her eyes are closed. After a while . . .

TOM: What did happen to your eye?

ANGELA *shrugs, not opening her eyes.*

Tell me.

ANGELA (*indifferently*): A guy came up behind me and threw me against a car.

TOM: Why? Who? (*He moves to make her look at him.*) Who?

ANGELA: A cop, I think. Out of uniform.

TOM (*his face hardening in fury*): Because you've been talking to me?

She shrugs, meaning "probably."

Exterior: Highbury Courthouse—Day

TOM is walking to the courthouse with purpose. He carries a briefcase. He runs up the stairs and in.

Interior: Courthouse Corridor—Day

TOM, striding along, comes to a door bearing a plaque marked "State's Attorney." He pushes it open and goes in. There is deadly purpose in his look.

Interior: Haggerty's Office—Day

Chief of Detectives BELLANCA *is seated at a table with* HAG-GERTY *and* TOM. *He is seething, openly contemptuous not only of* TOM *but of his boss as well.*

TOM (*to* HAGGERTY): I came to inform you that I have been retained on the Felix Daniels case to find new evidence for a retrial. I am asking for cooperation from the relevant personnel—I am not on a vendetta. I was a Boston cop for a lotta years.

BELLANCA (*cutting in*): Till they threw him out, I heard.

TOM: I made up my mind at breakfast that I'm not gonna get mad all day . . .

BELLANCA: Oh, give us a break, O'Toole. Who gives a shit if you get mad?

TOM: You never know, Chief.

BELLANCA (*to* HAGGERTY): I mean, Charley, you can't be seriously asking us to listen to this crap! I know the woman he's been talking to—that Angela Crispini.

TOM (*to* HAGGERTY): There is no question in my mind that Felix Daniels is innocent, and I want him out of jail.

BELLANCA: You finished?

TOM: Bellanca, you got the wrong man, and the smart thing would be to face it now.

BELLANCA (*stands, furious, addressing* HAGGERTY): The woman who is feedin' him this garbage has been a hooker for years! (*He counts on his fingers.*) The Highbury Inn, Looie's Forty-Eight Club, Ritchy's Truck Stop—you name it, she's hooked there, and he's taking her word against ours! (*To* TOM:) Felix Daniels killed his uncle Dr. Victor Daniels. Period.

BELLANCA *shoulders his way to the door and goes out.* TOM *seems slightly shaken but is still angry.*

HAGGERTY (*barely concealing his gladdened heart*): Okay ... this department will not obstruct any legitimate investigation of the Daniels case.

TOM: I will want to look at evidence.

HAGGERTY: If we've got it you can see it.

TOM: Right. (*He stands and goes to the door.*)

HAGGERTY: O'Toole?

TOM *turns.*

You will never get Daniels out, A. And B, this is the biggest mistake of your life. See you around.

TOM, *filled with anger and uncertainty, leaves fast.*

Exterior: Judge Murdoch's Estate—Day

Shotgun blasts shatter skeet discs. Backing, we find the shooter is Judge HARRY MURDOCH. *A former criminal lawyer of renown, he is now in his mid-sixties and in retirement has turned rosy and wise. He chews an unlit cigar and exudes success and contentment. There is a lot of vanity here, but also sentiment, when affordable. His attire is a gentleman farmer's.*

Behind him in the distance are the buildings of his rambling estate outside town. BILLY, *his driver and factotum, is operating the skeet-throwing machine.* TOM *stands to one side, admiring the judge's accuracy. He is carrying the transcript in a box under one arm.* MURDOCH *offers him the gun.*

MURDOCH: Try one?

TOM: Not my game. (*He hefts the box under his arm.*) Judge, when you can find a minute I've got the transcript of the Daniels case.

MURDOCH: Leave it with Jean. (*He takes a shot.*) What's that woman got to do with it—the one I saw you with? She the wife or something?

TOM: No, she's, ah . . . (*He laughs with some embarrassment.*) Tell you the God's honest truth, I'm still not sure what her connection is, but the case stinks, it really does, Judge. Charley Haggerty's turning into a public menace.

MURDOCH: No, no, he's just a second-rate mind in a position of power—the commonest story since the world began. (*He takes another shot.*) Are you sexually involved with this woman?

TOM: Well . . .

MURDOCH (*laughing*): No need to elaborate! (*He fires; another skeet shatters.*)

Interior: Angela's Bedroom—Afternoon

TOM *is just entering the room. She is sitting up in bed in a negligee, deeply absorbed in a book she simply can't tear herself away from.*

ANGELA: Be right with you. I know a wonderful pasta joint. You like ziti?

Tom: Couple of things we got to discuss, Angela, before we go out—I really have to.

Angela (*finally looking up at him*): God, you're a great-looking man. Have you read this? It's Joan Crawford's biography by her daughter.

Tom (*with a grin*): I'm not too big on trash.

Angela: Well, some trash is interesting, but I think it's uncalled-for. . . . I mean, her own *daughter.* My father raped me, but I'm not writing books about him.

Tom (*thrown*): Really raped you?

Angela: For years. By the same token, though, with people like him it wasn't, you know, all that unusual with a daughter. But it sure did *me* in.

Tom (*stares at her for a moment, then remembers his point*): Look, this is really important. We've got to get into some details about . . .

Angela: It's not important a woman was raped?

Tom (*openly impatient*): Now listen, Angela, it's out in the open that I'm on the case. . . . I have to know what your involvement is or I can't go ahead. (*He notes an inexplicable sort of tension coming over her, an internalized quality that walls her off from him.*)

Angela (*strained, highly anxious*): I told you. Victor Daniels was my *doctor* . . . (*Her breathing is deeper, flooding with anxiety. She clenches and unclenches her hands.*)

Tom: And Felix? You really never knew him before the trial?

Angela (*angrily offended*): I don't understand. You mean I can't be upset by an innocent man bein' put away?

TOM: Sure you can, but . . . listen, Angela, I am layin' my whole reputation on the line here. The least you can do is level with me! (*He breaks off, aware now of her metamorphosis.*)

ANGELA (*stands, her voice like gravel, her whole aspect transformed into that of a crude streetwalker*): C'mon, will ya, why don't you just come out with it!

> TOM *looks up at her, startled. She is strangely unloosened— one hip thrown out, arms akimbo, mouth distorted into a tough sneer.*

What you really mean is where does a fuckin' whore come off trying to . . .

TOM: Now wait, I didn't call you . . . that. (*He catches himself.*)

ANGELA: Go on, you're full of shit—you know I've been a hooker.

TOM: Angela, I—

ANGELA (*as though annoyed by a false name*): Screw this "Angela"! (*Cupping her breasts to thrust them forward, she taunts him.*) Grab onto this, you jerkoff choirboy. . . . Come on, get your fingers out of your yum-yum and try some of this!

TOM (*holding his head*): Holy God.

ANGELA: Go on, you don't kid me. (*She turns, trying to force his hand onto her buttocks.*) Grab hold, you fucking milk-face. You think you're better than anybody else?

TOM: Angela, Jesus . . .

> *They struggle; he forces her onto the bed. She screams, tries to fight him off, and loses her wind, gasping. He stands.*

She is clearly transported to another time and place. Her eyes are blind, he is a total stranger to her.

ANGELA: Well, if you can't get it up get goin'. I've got a line of guys into the street tonight. And the name is Leontine if you want to ask for me next time.

ANGELA has gradually lost an inner pressure and seems about to fall off to sleep. TOM bends over her, moved and mystified. He draws a blanket over her.

TOM: I'll drop by later. . . . Sleep now. I'll lock up.

She closes her eyes, sleeps. He takes a key out of her purse and stands looking around the room. He goes and picks up a photo of ANGELA accompanied by an unknown man, her momentary owner . . . (Is this Haggerty?) There's another photo on the wall with another man, this one on a snowy Vermont hotel porch. Finally he stares at the Virgin Mary on the wall over her bed. With a last perplexed if sympathetic glance at her, he lets himself out.

Exterior: Amy's House—Evening

TOM is approaching the house, which shows no light in the windows. He steps onto the porch and calls through the screen door.

TOM: Amy? You home?

He is coming back down the porch steps to return to his parked car when he sees a dim light inside the rusting wreck of a car with no doors. He looks in and discovers AMY; she is sitting on the back seat, dressed in jeans and a man's overlarge jacket. She has a couple of illustrated magazines on her lap and is reading under a kerosene lamp. At the same time she strokes a hen nesting on her lap.

TOM: Hiya, Amy.

AMY (*as though his appearance were perfectly ordinary*): Oh, hi.

TOM: Whatcha readin'?

AMY: About crocheting.

TOM: No kiddin'! You do crocheting?

AMY (*warmed by his interest, in her bleary way*): Maybe I'd take it up. 'Cause people would buy them.

TOM: Say, I'll bet! . . . Your friend Jerry wouldn't be around? I'd like to meet him.

AMY: He died once, you know. In Alabama someplace on his bike.

TOM: No! How'd that happen?

AMY: But he came back again. He might be over to the shop. I'm hungry.

TOM: Funny, I was just about to ask if you and Jerry would join me for a pizza.

AMY: Sure!

Interior: Mill Workshop—Tabernacle—Evening

AMY *is leading* TOM *through the courtyard to the shop.*

AMY: Hey, anybody around?

They pass into the workshop area, where MONTANA, *a clumsy beef of a fellow in a curled wide-brimmed Western hat and enormous moustache, is working on the engine of a motorbike.*

Hi, Montana, Jerry around?

MONTANA (*to* SONNY): Jerry around?

> SONNY *is also big but bald and sensitive, tending to shift from one foot to another when he stutters. He gestures toward the tabernacle.*

SONNY: I th-think he's w-w-welding in . . . I'll . . . t-t . . . (*He gives up trying to talk at all and gestures for* AMY *and* TOM *to follow.*)

> AMY *picks up one of the several stray kittens around the place.* SONNY *leads them through the open swinging plastic doors that connect the workshop to the tabernacle. They finally come upon* JERRY, *who is working on a large metal grid. He is kneeling, welding hubcaps to it.*
>
> *Like the other two men,* JERRY *has a forest simplicity in his gaze that makes his emotions hard to discover.* TOM *notes a ten-inch hunting knife sticking out of his boot top.* JERRY *is a longtime addict who is presently clear-eyed and on a health kick that he hopes will bring him closer to the mystery of creation and his own baffling guilt.*
>
> SONNY *brings them in. He speaks with a certain deference, as to a revered leader. He is loath to interrupt.*

SONNY: Jer! S-somebody . . . (*He gestures toward* TOM.)

AMY: He asked if he could buy us a pizza. (*She goes up to the improvised wooden stall in which a lamb is lying on some straw.*)

TOM: Hiya. . . . I'm Tom O'Toole, friend of Angela Crispini?

JERRY (*impatiently, to* AMY): Will you stop bothering those poor animals?

> JERRY *looks impatiently at* AMY, *whom he tends to treat roughly, but for whom he feels a certain tender pity. He registers Tom's presence but doesn't turn from his work.* TOM

approaches him cautiously and decides to press on despite the fact that JERRY *is ignoring him.*

TOM: Glad to meet you, Jerry. . . . Tell ya, I happened to be in the cemetery the other day, and I seen those burned bones layin' there. Angela says it's a . . . like a ritual. . . . I'm kind of interested in that stuff . . .

SONNY: You the c-cops?

JERRY: No, he's famous. I seen you once on the TV.

JERRY nods for SONNY *to get the hell out of there.* SONNY *moves off.*

TOM: Right. See, I am tryin' to help Angela . . .

Amy's kitten has managed to scramble free, and as she follows it, she accidentally dislodges a long tube of heavy steel standing propped up against the tabernacle screens.

JERRY doesn't see the tube falling. TOM, *with an automatic reaction, violently pushes* JERRY *out of its way as it bounces on the cement floor with a resonating clang.*

AMY screams. SONNY *stares at* JERRY, *fearing his reaction. There is a moment of tension between* JERRY *and* TOM.

TOM: Sorry to push you, but . . .

JERRY (*with suppressed excitement and a knowing little grin*): You *felt* that comin', didn't you? (*He turns and walks away.*)

Exterior: The Mill—Evening

It is a few minutes later. JERRY *sits on a piece of machinery, wiping his hands clean of oil.* TOM *approaches him cautiously. His instinct is not to speak yet but to communicate with him physically and try to draw him out that way.*

AMY (*to* JERRY, *more desperately*): He wants to buy us a pizza, okay?

JERRY (*ignoring her, to* TOM): Trouble with Angela is she can't communicate. She can't unload.

TOM (*as naively as he is able*): You think that's what she wants to do?

JERRY: It's what everybody wants to do—tell it, get rid of it, put it behind you. The Major could help, but she won't let him.

> SONNY *and* MONTANA *move into the shot. Their arrival creates the feeling of a séance as they listen intently.*

AMY: He was almost a priest.

TOM (*alerted*): Say, that's right. You're Catholic, aren't you?

JERRY: I wasn't normal enough for the priesthood—kept tryin' to get out over the wall to find girls.

> TOM *decides not to push him on this.*

I saw Jesus once. But he never come back. But the Major's there, man, he's *there.* 'Course Angela's got nobody . . . so she keeps going off that way.

AMY: Can't we eat?

TOM: Goin' off how, Jerry?

JERRY (*rises, starts walking back into the workshop*): Changin' herself into this one and that one. You've seen her do that, haven't you? That's nothin' but psychic possession. That's never going to get her clear.

TOM: Clear of what, Jerry? What do you think is grabbing her?

JERRY (*sharpening his knife on a grinder as sparks fly*): You been to seminary, haven't you.

TOM: Funny you ask that. . . . No, but I've got a brother in the church.

JERRY: I knew it. (*He shakes his head in wonder, with a glimmer of warmth now.*) Can always tell.

SONNY (*strolls up, winding himself up to say something*): J-J-Jerry—

JERRY (*turning on him sharply*): I'm *talkin'* to this man!

> SONNY *stops obediently.* JERRY *turns his back on him. He wipes the knife clean and shows it to* TOM.

Major give me this. People don't believe it, but he did. Read that?

TOM (*reads the inscription on the knife*): "Grand Army of the Republic." Huh! And he give you this?

JERRY (*nods*): His battle knife from the Civil War. . . . You believe it?

TOM: Why not?

> AMY *moves into the shot.* JERRY *never takes his fascinated eyes from* TOM.

AMY: Don't I ever get to eat today! I'm hungry!

TOM: How about a pizza? Let's go to Giorgio's, my treat.

JERRY (*again with suppressed excitement, which he tries to hold down*): Meet you there. (*He walks off,* AMY *trailing behind.*)

Establishing Shot: Pizza Parlor/Diner

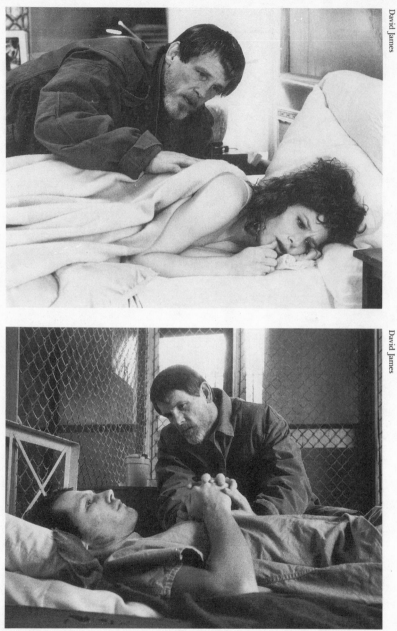

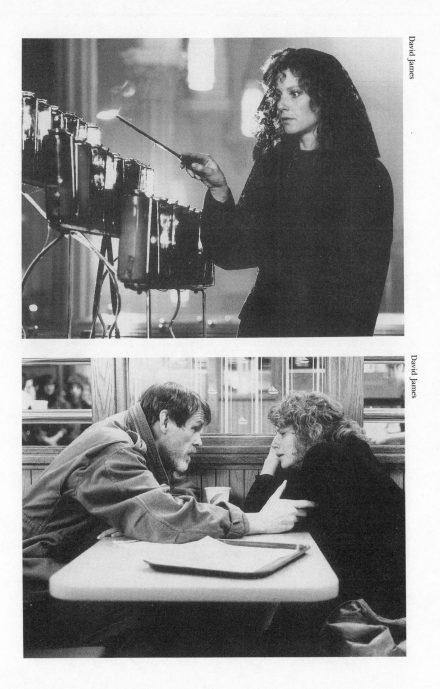

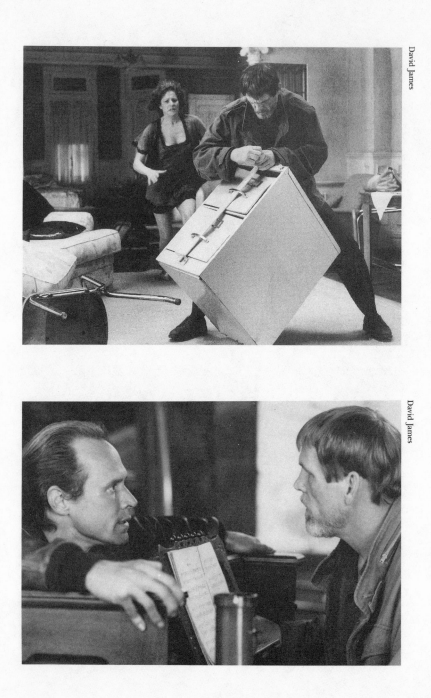

Interior: Pizza Parlor/Diner—Evening

The place is nearly empty. There's been a pause in the conversation. JERRY *and* TOM *watch* AMY *as she ravenously gorges the last of a large pizza.* JERRY *gently straightens her hair.*

JERRY: She backfired once and never been the same. I've got myself pretty straightened out, see, but I'm . . . I'm still kind of loaded up a lot of the time.

TOM: I'm reading you, Jerry.

JERRY: I know. I knew it soon as you looked at me. But it's . . . (*sighing, shaking his head*) . . . so hard.

TOM (*lets a moment pass*): That shows you're not an animal, don't it, Jerry? I mean, there's lots that wouldn't be bothered, right?

JERRY: I can't hardly breathe sometimes.

AMY: 'Cause there's some other people involved, see . . .

JERRY (*eyes flaring, wraps his knuckles on top of her head as if on a door*): You got anything in there? What you got in there!

JERRY *has knocked* AMY *off her chair. She's crying,* JERRY *is upset. He lifts her to her feet with a strangely tender touch.*

Exterior: Pizza Parlor/Diner—Evening

JERRY *is on his motorbike and has just kick-started it.* AMY *is riding behind him with her cheek nuzzling his shoulder.*

TOM *is handing* JERRY *a card.*

TOM: That's my number, day or night. . . . I'll be by again in a day or two, okay?

TOM *pushes the card into Jerry's pocket.* JERRY *revs his bike.* TOM *holds him back.*

Guess I don't have to tell you, Jerry—there's no power in the world can break a man's grip on his own throat.

JERRY *nods with recognition. Fear and hope are struggling in his gaze.*

But you know who can, don't you?

JERRY *doesn't reply. He rides off on the motorbike.*

Interior: Angela's Apartment—Night

TOM *is approaching quietly from the door, not sure if* AN-GELA's *awake. He is taking his coat off.*

ANGELA (*off screen*): Tom, is that you?

Interior: Angela's Bedroom—Same Time

ANGELA *lies down on the bed.* TOM *sits on the edge and covers her. She lowers her eyes contritely and speaks in a whisper. Her secret is out.*

TOM: Looks like you slept.

ANGELA: I felt safe. I'm sorry, I should have leveled with you, but I wasn't sure you'd understand.

He waits. She takes a breath.

I'm a . . . I come apart. I . . . like, break up.

TOM: Are you under psychiatric care?

ANGELA: I used to be, but I haven't had any episodes in

about three years. But it doesn't mean I don't tell you the truth.

TOM: It's just that the way you suddenly come at me just before . . . and in Jerry's place . . .

ANGELA (*with a clear flowering of anxious uncertainty*): Jerry's place? What did I say in Jerry's place?

TOM: That I mustn't go tracking anybody without your say-so.

ANGELA: Who was I talking about?

TOM (*amazed that she doesn't remember*): This Jerry who everybody says killed Victor Daniels.

ANGELA (*trying to penetrate the fog, alarmed*): *Jerry?* . . . Oh, right. That's because I don't want you to ever be alone with him. He can get crazy, you know . . .

TOM: I just been with Jerry. Talking to him.

He stops right there, intending her to see that he has not obeyed her and is awaiting her next move. ANGELA *lies back on the pillow, in conflict as she looks up at him.*

You want to go to sleep, or you want to talk?

She can't decide what to say to him—the bridge of trust has now to be crossed, or not.

Am I wrong? I have the feeling you want to tell me something.

There is a submerged warning in that last sentence. ANGELA *is visibly filling with emotion as she looks at him. She lifts his hand and kisses it reverently, sets it back, and chastely removes her own hand. Moved by the torture he senses in her, he takes her hand and kisses it. Tears spring to her eyes.*

ANGELA: Tom?

TOM (*having crossed one bridge now*): Yes.

ANGELA: I used to be with Victor.

TOM: *Victor Daniels?* I thought he was such a pillar.

ANGELA (*staring straight up at him*): He saved me. He paid all
my doctor's bills. (*As though taking a vow, solemnly:*) I will
always owe Victor.

TOM (*deeply stirred*): Must've been some shock then, huh.

ANGELA: Butchered. And the killer right there advertising
himself, and they go and put Felix away. . . . Listen, I want
to talk to you for days, but I have to feel we're friends.

TOM: I have to say it—I've never known anybody it was so
hard to get a fix on.

ANGELA (*feeling slightly released, smiling*): Well, I've got a lot of
sides, but that makes it more interesting, doesn't it? (*As
though unable to hold back any longer, she suddenly comes up off
her pillow and, grasping his face, kisses him on the mouth with a
strangely determined desperation.*) Oh, Tom, I need you!

Exterior: Riverbank—Day

Close shot: TOM *is sitting in his car beside the river, amid trees
and brush. Looking through his binoculars, he sees a big
truck in the mill courtyard.*

Under Jerry's supervision, SONNY *and* MONTANA *are slid-
ing a large object out of the truck down two planks.* AMY *is
watching. A police car is parked nearby.* BELLANCA'S SIDE-
KICK *is leaning against it smoking, casually observing the
activity as if joking with friends.*

They manage to slide the object to the ground. It's a small upright harmonium. JERRY *motions for* AMY *to try it out, and while* MONTANA *pumps away, Amy starts playing.*

After a while, with the music floating faintly across the river, JERRY *performs a kind of jig, and the others, including the cop, start clapping.* TOM *can't help smiling, shaking his head in puzzlement.*

Exterior: Judge Murdoch's Estate—Day

We see an imposing white building with sloping tiered lawns overlooking the town. TOM *is purposefully climbing the steep steps that lead to the portico. A German shepherd runs at him, barking.* JEAN, *the judge's secretary, opens the front door and calls to the dog.*

JEAN: Rupert!

The dog subsides.

TOM (*coming up*): Thanks, Jean. (*He gives her a quick kiss.*) What are you doing working on Saturday?

JEAN (*smiling*): Catching up on the mail. (*She shows him in.*) He's in the billiard room. He's through for the day.

TOM *goes in, and* JEAN *closes the door behind him.*

Interior: Judge Murdoch's House—Billiard Room—Day

Judge MURDOCH *is in shirtsleeves, expertly playing pool with* TOM, *but his suit and vest suggest he's spent the day in town. On the wall behind him are photos of him with Ed Sullivan, Eisenhower, Stevenson, Reagan, etc.*

MURDOCH: Incidentally . . . I'm not supposed to be saying this yet, but your friend Charley Haggerty looks like the party's choice for the Senate this time.

TOM: The Senate! You're killing me!

MURDOCH: Well, he's no worse a meathead than a lot of other meatheads. But this time he's not going down easy. He'll fight for his life on this case.

TOM: I reversed him once, and I can do it again.

MURDOCH: Tom, what if I told you that I'm beginning to wonder if you ought to forget the whole thing?

TOM: You're not serious.

MURDOCH: This woman is your entire case, and you still can't tell me why she's even involved.

TOM: I'm still trying to dig it out of her. But I will, I know I will.

MURDOCH: Listen to me, Tommy—if she won't come clean, you have got to take a walk. This is basic, kid.

TOM: I know it!

MURDOCH: You keep saying that, but what is her connection? I get the feeling you're walking on bubbles!

TOM: I'm ashamed of myself—you're right. I been letting my dingus do my thinking. But don't worry, it's not that serious . . .

MURDOCH: All sex is serious! Specially with romantic fellows like you. You guys always idealize the woman you're screwing. You better stay out of her bed. (*He goes to a table, picks up the trial transcript, and hands it to* TOM.) I read this.

TOM: And?

MURDOCH: She's got a right to be upset. (*He points at the transcript.*) All they proved in court was that Felix was in the doctor's house. Nobody proved he killed anybody.

TOM (*fears gone, depression over, almost shouting with revived indignation*): Then I *am* right! Haggerty did it again!

MURDOCH: But you've got to nail that woman's story. *Evidence,* not bubbles! *Where is she coming from?*

Interior: Angela's Apartment—Night

The door is just being unlocked from within, and we hear Angela's voice.

ANGELA (*off screen*): Right with you!

TOM (*enters and talks toward the half-open bathroom door, full of determination now*): Look, Angela . . . you have got to sit down with me and concentrate on some answers. I've got a list of questions as long as your leg, so how about we get down to it right away?

ANGELA (*stepping out of the bathroom in slacks, high heels, nifty blouse, and bandanna*): Ta-da! I want to go bowling.

TOM (*incredulously*): You *what?*

Exterior: Bowling Alley—Night

TOM *and* ANGELA *emerge from Tom's car and walk to the bowling alley entrance. He grasps her arm and stops her.*

TOM: Okay, we bowl for an hour. Then we eat—and talk.

ANGELA: Absolutely! I promise. Stop being so serious all the time.

Interior: Bowling Alley—Night

TOM *is just sending a ball down the alley. It drifts to one side and knocks down only a couple of pins.* ANGELA *picks up her ball and sights the pins.*

Three BOWLERS *enter, seating themselves at the adjoining alley. They are middle-aged types who instantly recognize her.*

BOWLER 1: Go get him, Swede!

She grins at him with a laugh, in her element here. TOM *catches their familiarity and smiles uncomfortably.*

BOWLER 2: Down the middle, Angie!

ANGELA: Shut up, will ya? Gimme a break, I'm trying to concentrate!

BOWLER 3 (*approaches her rather unsteadily, roaring as he yanks open a beer*): Concentrate on this, baby! (*He squirts her with beer.*)

ANGELA (*protesting but laughing, pleased at being the center of attention*): Vincent, for Christ's sake!

BOWLER 3 (*wiping her off and feeling far down on her ass*): Ohhh . . . I'm sorry, honey . . .

ANGELA (*slaps his hand away, still laughing*): Get out of there, you . . .

BOWLER 3 *persists, laughing with her, and his hand returns to her ass. She doesn't swipe it away this time.* TOM *begins to move in.*

TOM: Hey, fella, the woman asked you not to go bothering her . . .

ANGELA (*instantly blocking* TOM): He doesn't mean anything. . . . Here, sit down. Now, watch me.

> TOM *allows her to seat him, but his face fills the lens—he has a new awareness of her real life.*

TOM: Okay, let's see you bowl.

> ANGELA *bends for her shot.* TOM *looks to the three* BOWLERS *and back to her. She bowls a strike. The* BOWLERS *roar out their cheers, and she faces them with arms triumphantly raised, leaving* TOM *quite out of it.*
>
> *Close shot: An angry, hurt look deepens on Tom's face.*
>
> *Fade out.*
>
> *Fade in:*

> *Exterior: Tom's House and Land—Morning*
>
> *Close on* TOM *as he fiercely hurls an old baseball across the stubbled winter pasture. His dog gallops after the ball, which is rolling toward the house.* TOM *walks after the dog. From the house we hear the faint ring of a telephone: once, twice, then it stops.* TOM *moves faster.*

> *Interior: Tom's Kitchen—Morning*
>
> TOM *comes into the kitchen, where* CONNIE *is making breakfast.*

TOM: I heard the phone.

CONNIE: It was her.

TOM: Why didn't you call me?

CONNIE: She'll call back.

TOM: You knew I was outside! Why didn't you call me!

CONNIE *won't answer.* TOM *restrains himself with effort.*

Next time you call me!

CONNIE: Don't talk to me that way! I'm not your servant!

Interior: Tom's Dining Room—Later

CONNIE *and* TOM *have calmed down, but she is still unhappy.*

CONNIE (*resolute now*): Tom . . . listen. I'm really wondering whether I ought to stay on . . .

TOM (*incredulous and put-out*): What're you talking about?

CONNIE: I don't feel comfortable living here with all this going on.

TOM: With what going on?

CONNIE (*embarrassed*): Oh, for heaven's sake. I've heard all the stories about that woman.

He can't bring himself to dispute this.

I came here because you and the boys needed me when they were in school, but now you ought to lead your life the way you want . . .

TOM: Connie! There's a kid in jail and she's got the key! (*Her doubting look presses him on.*) Even Judge Murdoch thinks he's innocent. And he's read the transcript!

CONNIE: And how do you know she's not making it with him?

TOM: Oh, come on!

The phone rings. TOM *rises to answer it.*

CONNIE: Why not? From what I hear, it's her way of saying hello.

TOM: She's not that bad . . . (*into phone*) . . . yeah? Jerry! Hey, good to hear you. What's happening? . . . (*He is joyfully surprised.*) Oh, I'd be happy to. . . . Sure, I can make it this morning. Certainly. See you right away. (*Incredulous, he hangs up and turns to* CONNIE.) Our boy Jerry! Wants to talk to me right away! (*He grasps both her hands as though about to dance with her.*)

CONNIE *is half carried along, but only half, and with an unwilling laugh cuffs him on the cheek.*

Interior: The Mill—Workshop—Tabernacle—Day

AMY *is pumping away at the old harmonium, playing a hymn with lots of wrong notes.*

The building of the tabernacle has progressed a little. Wooden crates have been placed in position like pews around an altar.

SONNY *and* MONTANA *are placing one of the reflecting screens in position around the altar. These are steel mesh decorated with chrome hubcaps like ancient warriors' shields.* JERRY *is supervising the work.*

TOM (*indicating all the activity*): You really got these boys pitchin' in. You're going to end up with a beautiful church here.

JERRY: They used to be all strung out, you know.

TOM: You saved them.

JERRY (*with a deep nod*): The Major and me.

TOM (*lets this pass for the moment*): You wanted to talk to me, Jerry?

JERRY (*nods, then pauses, inwardly struggling*): I want to . . . I want to help Angela.

TOM: Help? How?

JERRY: Her brains are choking. She's very bad, you know.

TOM: Oh, don't I know.

JERRY: Her thoughts are poisoning her. But she won't—you know, trust me enough. Maybe if you sat down with us, just us three . . . we could—you know, talk.

TOM: Sure, be happy to. (*Mystified but encouraged, he is quietly trying to read the ulterior purpose here; he nods for an instant.*) I'll get right on it. (*He starts to leave, pausing over* AMY, *who is still at the harmonium.*) How's it goin', Amy?

She raises one hand in acknowledgment, looking up at him with her unfocused stare.

See ya, honey. (*He strides off with anticipatory excitement.*)

Exterior: Angela's Apartment—Night

The camera is shooting through Angela's bedroom window. She walks up to it, playing with an unlit cigarette. She stares out, a brooding look of tension on her face. Behind her, TOM *is pacing up and down the room, talking.*

Interior: Angela's Bedroom—Same Time

Tom *is still pacing.*

Tom: . . . The man is winding himself up to come clean—
I'm telling you my instinct. He's on the point of cracking
open. He wants you to hold his hand.

*He comes to stand behind her now and gently eases the
cigarette out of her fingers. She lets him do it but walks away to
sit on the bed.*

What are you afraid of? I'll be right there with you.

Angela: You like me a little?

Tom: A little!

Angela (*closes her eyes*): I want to hear it.

Tom (*takes her in his arms*): You're the most unexpected thing
ever happened to me.

Her eyes remain closed. He looks at her.

I'm with you, honey. Why can't you trust me?

Her eyes open, and he senses her softening.

I'm with you all the way. Can't you tell me the story? Just
start anywhere and tell me.

Angela (*after a last hesitation*): Jerry was a runner.

Tom *waits for her to go on.*

He ran drugs for Victor.

Tom (*astounded*): Dr. Daniels was in drugs?

Angela: He was the main man.

Tom: Boy, I'm really out of it—that never crossed my mind. (*He thinks, trying to fit this new information in with the rest.*) But why did Jerry kill Daniels?

Angela: Victor owed him money. Jerry'd got this crazy idea that Victor had to help him build a church, and he wouldn't do it. . . . Jerry went berserk . . .

Tom: Why didn't the cops arrest him?

Angela: He knows all the connections.

Tom: Connections to . . .

Angela: Drugs and the police—Bellanca.

Tom: How come they didn't just waste him?

Angela: Maybe they will.

Tom: You mean if he keeps talking to me.

Angela *nods, silent.*

Well . . . it all suddenly makes sense. And I can see why you always seem so terrified—

Her helplessness moves him. He takes her hand: a moment of tenderness. He glances over to a framed photo standing on a table with several others.

Close shot: Photo of Angela *on a motorboat, in a bikini, posing spread out on the open deck, with a gangster type in sunglasses behind her.*

Is that Bimini?

She nods.

Amy says now and then she and you would donkey the stuff up from there.

ANGELA: I stopped two years ago. (*She genuinely weeps for a ruined life.*)

TOM (*holds her close*): The cops must know about that.

> *She nods.*

So how do you come to be beatin' on them with this case now?

ANGELA: Because I know how innocent Felix is, and I can't bear it.

> *He lets this sink in. Suddenly he's galvanized: he has the story, and he sees the answer.*

TOM: We'll go meet Jerry, talk, and get this over with. (*He rises and goes to get her coat.*)

ANGELA (*not moving*): Tom. I have to tell you something.

TOM: Tell me in the car.

ANGELA (*with a flash of resentment*): I am trying to tell you something!

> *He stops.*

I used to be with Charley Haggerty.

TOM (*resolved not to be taken in—this seems total madness*): You were in the hammock with the prosecutor?

> *She barely nods; it is a confession with suffering attached. He is straight-faced, but doubt remains in his tone.*

ANGELA: He nearly left his wife for me.

TOM: No kiddin'.

ANGELA: The best two years of my life. Until they made him rig the case against Felix.

TOM: Why'd they make him do it?

ANGELA: A man as important as Dr. Daniels chopped up like that . . . they had to nail it on somebody, and Jerry was absolutely out. Jerry could bomb the whole police department plus both parties in this town in the bargain. This case goes to the top of the mountain, Tom, the *top*.

> *She gets up, moving now with the verve and energy of one released, acting out the story.* TOM *watches, mesmerized, trying to pierce the truth of this outrageous yet circumstantially convincing story.*

We'd go to Charley's place on the beach and sit staring at the fire. . . . It was killing him. I'd plead with him: "You could be anything, Charley, you could end up president of the United States, but you can't do this to an innocent man."

> *A new mood now: she is flooded with a mixture of indignation and fear. Her breathing deepens. And now* TOM *tries to break into the center.*

TOM: If we can get Jerry to unload in front of a lawyer, you've not only sprung that innocent kid, I've nailed the police department and Haggerty. . . . I think you owe Felix that much.

ANGELA: You can't let Jerry loose in a courtroom. (*Suddenly she is totally unconnected to him, moving about frantically, terrified and furious. Her breathing comes harder and harder.*) Don't be telling me who I owe! I've done more for Felix than you or anyone else.

Tom: Why won't you come with me to Jerry! Answer me, goddamn you!

Angela (*suddenly stiffening in an image of the highest female dignity*): I must say, you are terribly irritating.

Tom: Oh, Jesus, not *that* song and dance again!

Angela (*with a remote inward stare that tells how far into this new character she has fled*): What astounds me is how you get to think you're such a high-grade cultured individual and such a great Catholic . . .

Tom: In other words, this whole story has been bullshit!

Angela: . . . when all you really are is guttural!

Tom: You're not even using that word right!

Angela: Your whole manner is guttural because your whole background is guttural!

Tom (*spreading his arms*): Okay, Renata, pull out the nails! I want to come down.

Angela: You can call me Miss Sherwood, you stupid bastard.

Tom: Miss Renata Sherwood ought to know that high-class, respectable ladies don't call people stupid bastards.

Angela: Which I would be delighted to do if these stupid bastards had the competence to understand any other kind of language, you dumb shit!

Tom: Touché!

She plunks down on the bed, nearly exhausted.

And, lady, you just convinced me from this minute that you don't know a goddamn thing about this case, and you never laid a hand on Charley Haggerty except in your misbegotten dreams!

This hits ANGELA *like a physical blow. She is stunned. After a moment, without looking at him, she rises, as if with some undeclared purpose. She goes toward the far end of the apartment as if to walk out the door.*

Where are you going?

She doesn't answer. She goes to a cupboard, opens a drawer, and takes out a scuffed, bulging envelope. Without speaking, she throws it on the floor in front of TOM. *She moves away.*

Close-up: The envelope is full of mementos of Angela's life with HAGGERTY. *Pasted on the outside is a clipping from the local newspaper.* HAGGERTY *is standing, hands in the air in a victory salute, surrounded by congratulatory people. A headline proclaims his victory in a recent election.*

TOM *pulls a photograph from the envelope at random. It's a version of the photo we have already seen.* ANGELA *is sitting on the man's shoulders, but here we can see his face clearly. It's* HAGGERTY. *He and* ANGELA *are laughing.*

TOM *turns to look at her. She's coming out of her dressing room, carrying a small jewelry box. She lobs it underhand to* TOM, *who catches it and opens the lid. Inside is a diamond ring.*

Interior: Tom's House—Night

Long shot: Tom's living room is in darkness. TOM *walks into the empty room and goes to his office, turning on only the light above his desk. He doesn't want to wake* CONNIE. *He's wearing his overcoat.*

Without taking it off, he sits down. He takes something out of his pocket.

Close-up: A strip of snapshots from an "instant photo" machine shows ANGELA *and* HAGGERTY *horsing around, two playful lovers.*

Nearby the answering machine's message light is blinking. TOM *turns it to playback. He picks up a magnifying glass and holds it over the snapshots.*

RECORDED VOICE: This is Father Mancini. I'm chaplain at the correctional facility. I have rather disturbing news about Felix Daniels. . . .

TOM *studies the enlarged, distorted images in the magnifying glass as he listens.*

RECORDED VOICE (*Father* MANCINI, *continuing*): I think you could be of some help. Could you give me a ring? The number is 594-0077.

The message ends, the machine beeps. There's a second message.

RECORDED VOICE (*impatient, angry*): Ray Smith—Northern Hazard. You said you were going to call us Monday.

TOM *turns off the machine, thinks for a moment, then pushes the photo into an empty business envelope.*

Interior: Penitentiary Corridor—Holding Cells—Day

Father MANCINI, *a young, intense priest, is leading* TOM *along a busy prison corridor toward a door to a walkway.*

MANCINI: It's good of you to do this, Mr. O'Toole.

The walkway is one floor above the holding cells. From there they can look down and see FELIX *in one of the cells. He's lying on a cot, covered with a thin flannel sheet.* TOM *starts down toward him, and* MANCINI *goes back the way they came.*

Interior: Holding Cell—Day

Close on a plastic tray with a hospital-type water jug, paper cups, and an untouched bowl of something like banana pudding.

TOM *is sitting on a stool next to Felix's cot. He pours some water into a paper cup. Pale and deathly,* FELIX *stares at the ceiling.*

TOM: Take some water. Come on, Felix.

TOM *offers the cup, but* FELIX *indicates he doesn't want it.* TOM *keeps it extended.*

You've got to hold on, Felix. You can't get too discouraged—it's not going to go on forever, like you think. You don't know me. I have my minuses, but I never let go. I'm gaining on this every day. You are definitely going to walk out of here, you understand?

He offers FELIX *the cup again.* FELIX *accepts it and takes a swallow of water.*

I want you to start eating, you hear? Get your strength back. Focus your thoughts . . . I'll be back in a week, okay? I'm going to have news for you. . . . Felix?

FELIX *turns his face to the wall. Tom's face reflects his heightened anxiety.*

Interior: Prison Office Connecting to Visitors' Room—Day

TOM *comes in looking for* MANCINI *and sees him talking to a* PRISONER *in the visitors' room.* MANCINI *excuses himself to the* PRISONER *and comes into the office.*

TOM: He wouldn't say a word.

MANCINI: What matters is seeing you. He needs to know there's somebody on his side. He trusts you, Mr. O'Toole. You will be back, I hope . . .

TOM: I told him I would be.

> *They're both aware of the* PRISONER *waiting for* MANCINI. *The priest moves to leave, then turns back to* TOM.

MANCINI: We should talk further. How about this evening, after the seven o'clock mass? At St. Jude's?

TOM: Sure, Father.

> MANCINI *goes back to the visitors' room, and* TOM *leaves the office.*

Interior—St. Jude's Catholic Church—Night

A service is in progress, an ordinary weekday evening mass. The camera closes on TOM *as he enters at the back of the church, automatically dipping his fingers in the holy water font to cross himself. He continues forward, then stops.*

Tom's point of view: He is near the altar, where Father MAN-CINI *is distributing Communion to a few worshipers at the rail. Among them is* ANGELA, *wearing a lacy scarf.*

When MANCINI *comes to* ANGELA, *his face softens. She tilts her head back for the Host, opening her mouth, her eyes fixed on his, in an intense exchange of feeling with the innocent, fascinated young priest.*

Close-up: Tom's face registers shock, amazement.

Tom's point of view: ANGELA *leaves the rail and returns to her pew.* MANCINI, *with a certain passion, looks after her for a moment before turning to proceed with the rest of the mass.*

Interior: St. Jude's Sacristy—Minutes Later

Father MANCINI *is removing his vestments as he talks to* TOM. *He has left the door open, and from there they can see back into the church.*

They're both watching ANGELA. *She has left the pew and moved to a side altar with a statue of the Virgin and a bank of votive candles. She lights a candle and kneels in prayer.*

MANCINI: Angela's spoken about you so often. I'm glad we've met.

TOM: She's talked about you too, Father. You're her favorite fella in the whole world.

MANCINI: Not quite. I think you are.

TOM *looks at him. There's a moment of silence between them.* MANCINI *is up to something.* TOM *is uncomfortable.*

MANCINI: She's terribly worried, you know, that you may give up on this case. I hope you're not, are you?

TOM: I don't know . . . (*He looks back toward* ANGELA.)

Tom's point of view: ANGELA *has finished her prayers and is going off through the church.*

TOM (*off screen*): I would if I could.

The camera returns to TOM *and* MANCINI.

TOM (*looking at* MANCINI *a little harder now*): Did she ask you to talk to me?

Mancini's look is evasive, ambiguous.

Did she?

MANCINI: Mr. O'Toole, you are her lifeline now. You are all that connects her to life. I hope and pray you know that.

TOM, *with a faint movement, acknowledges that he heard. He starts walking away.*

MANCINI: Mr. O'Toole . . . life sometimes brings us angels unforeseen.

TOM *nods his head and walks off.*

Interior: Tom's Bedroom—Night

TOM *is asleep. The illuminated clock beside the bed reads 11:30 p.m. The phone rings—a short, abbreviated ring. *TOM* wakes. Silence. He turns to go back to sleep, then hears Connie's raised voice from her bedroom, across the hall. He lifts the phone and hears . . .*

CONNIE (*voice-over, on phone, vehemently*): You whore, stop trying to destroy this man!

TOM (*into phone*): Angela? (*But the line is dead.*) Angela!

He hangs up and rushes into Connie's room. She is getting out of bed.

You must never do that again!

CONNIE *grabs her dressing gown and heads out the door that leads to the main room.*

CONNIE: I'm leaving, I can't stay here. Not with whores calling up in the middle of the night.

TOM *follows her. She's wildly searching the dining room table for her cigarettes. The packs are empty.*

TOM: Now stop this, you hear me!

CONNIE: She's a whore, isn't she? You knew that when you met her!

TOM (*defensively*): It's not that simple. There's a lot more to it than that . . .

CONNIE (*in deep spiritual alarm, her hands clasped before her*): What is happening to you!

TOM: I don't know what is happening to me, Connie. All I can tell you is that I am breaking this case, whatever it takes . . .

CONNIE (*her resistance crumbling*): I don't know you anymore!

TOM (*with a certain brutal edge*): *Whatever it takes!*

Exterior: Tom's House—A Little Later

The night is moonlit. Through a window we can see CONNIE *sitting at the dining table, her head in her hands.* TOM *comes up to her, bringing a cup of hot milk. He sets it in front of her.*

Interior: Tom's House—Same Time

CONNIE *picks up the cup to drink, and* TOM *sits down beside her.*

TOM: We weren't taught for this world, Connie, and I don't like it any better than you do. (*He gets up and starts pacing.*) But I'm not going under. I don't think I am, anyway. Trust me. 'Cause I really do need you, Connie. Okay?

She can barely nod her assent, moved by her love rather than her understanding.

Please, now . . . go to sleep, huh?

CONNIE (*stands, speaking quietly, conceding*): Call her back if you want. She sounded like she was in trouble. (*She leaves the room.*)

Exterior: Burger King—Night

The place is open, though the streets are empty. Tom's car roars into the parking lot. TOM *jumps out.*

Interior: Burger King—Same Time

It's after 2:00 a.m. and the place is busy. ANGELA *wears sunglasses.*

TOM: Can I see it?

She hesitates for a moment, then lowers her glasses. She has a bruise on her upper lid.

You want to talk about it?

She goes back to eating.

Was it the cops?

ANGELA (*gets set to speak, but it isn't easy*): Haggerty.

TOM: Charley Haggerty beat you up? (*He can't keep the skepticism out of his voice, and yet . . .*) Where? Why? Talk to me, will you?

ANGELA: He came to get his letters back.

TOM: What letters?

ANGELA: I'm scared to death, Tom.

TOM (*grips her hand*): You have letters from him?

> *She nods.*

You mean like love letters?

ANGELA (*nods*): And about the case. One of them.

TOM: Actually referring to it?

ANGELA: Asking me not to let it get between us. Because of what he had to do.

TOM: Did you give them to him?

ANGELA: No.

TOM: My God, Angela! If you got something like that—it could wrap it all up.

ANGELA: But it would destroy him.

TOM: Well? . . . (*His voice implies "Why not?"*)

ANGELA: I can't bear to do that to him. I'm only telling you so you'll see my problem.

TOM: What problem? Honey, he is the chief law enforcement officer of this county, and he knowingly rigs a murder case? He's gotta be destroyed.

ANGELA (*feeling her anguish rejected*): How can I do that! He was the love of my life!

TOM *glances away to suppress an outburst.*

Exterior: Parking Lot—Moments Later

The lot is empty but for Tom's car. TOM and ANGELA are getting in. Traffic is going by on the adjacent highway.

Interior: Tom's Car—Same Time

TOM: A man who takes his fists to a woman ought to be strung up by his testicles.

ANGELA: He lost his temper for a minute. He's just immature.

TOM: He come with cops?

ANGELA: No, alone. But I'm afraid he might come back.

TOM (*turns her to face him, speaking decisively*): You want out of this? Or you want to go on being treated like shit? . . . Answer me, what do you want?

ANGELA (*struggling with herself*): Out.

TOM: Then let me take you home right now. You give me one of his letters, and we finish the case . . . and you can start living like a human being, okay?

ANGELA (*shuts her eyes, her fear continuing*): Okay.

TOM *starts the car and drives quickly out of the parking lot.*

Exterior: Angela's Street—Night

Tom's car comes to a halt before her house.

Interior: Tom's Car—Same Time

TOM *shuts off the engine. For a moment* ANGELA *doesn't move.*

TOM: Come on. Let's do it.

ANGELA *nods her head. She has been grasping the key in her hand. She gives it to him. They walk into the house.*

Interior: Angela's Apartment—Moments Later

The place has been wrecked. TOM *is outraged as he looks around. On the floor lies the four-drawer steel file cabinet, its iron bar intact along the front, secured by the heavy padlock. It shows signs of having been attacked, metal bent. With effort he rights the file.*

ANGELA *looks on with mounting terror as he reaches into his pocket, takes out the key . . . and suddenly she is on him.*

ANGELA (*nearly screaming*): No! Give it to me! (*She pulls at his hand.*)

TOM: What the hell you doing?

He pushes her away, but she is back in an instant, with the energy of terror.

ANGELA: You tricked me! Give it back to me, it's mine!

She bites his hand, and in his pain he sends her banging up against a wall. But again she is back at him, clawing at his hand, until with a hard slap to the side of her head he raps her down on the bed, his knee in her belly.

That's my property. . . . You're a goddamn thief! I want my property! I'll go to the cops . . . tell 'em you stole my property!

His eyes light up. He releases her and steps away, out of breath.

TOM: You called me in to dig up just enough to get Felix out, is that it? But without touching anybody else! Is that the story? And now you're asking me to protect the bastard who put him in there?

He pushes both his arms back and forth in opposite directions. She is bent over, rocking in frustration.

You been trying to go north and south and powder your nose all at the same time! (*He laughs viciously.*) But it can't be done, baby—not with me!

She straightens up from her crouch, and with a cry from her gut she slides to her knees on the floor.

ANGELA: *Help me!*

He looks down at her abjectly pleading face. He tosses the key to the floor in front of her.

TOM (*resisting pity*): Okay. You give me one sentence in a letter from Haggerty and I'm your man. Otherwise, you been full of shit from day one and *I am out of your life!*

Jaws clenched in conflict, she struggles with herself. He stands there watching her, refusing to crumble before her need, struggling to keep from rushing in again to assuage her pain—waiting for her, in effect, to break.

He walks out.

Exterior: Angela's House—Dawn

Outside the house, TOM gets into his car and drives off furiously down the hill. A motorcycle with an unidentified rider (SONNY) appears and follows him.

Exterior: Town Square—Dawn

High angle: Tom's car speeds through the empty square, still followed by the motorcycle.

Interior: Tom's Car—Dawn

Close-up: TOM is driving fast through town, along the deserted streets.

Insert: The rearview mirror reflects the motorcycle following Tom's car, flashing its headlight at him.

Exterior: Deserted Street—Dawn

High angle: As Tom's car turns a corner, the motorcycle catches up and is about to overtake it when TOM brakes violently and comes to a stop. The motorcycle circles the car and stops by Tom's window. SONNY raps on the glass.

Interior: Tom's Car—Dawn

TOM *rolls down the window, and* SONNY *leans close.*

SONNY (*anguished*): I been l-l-lookin' for y-you. (*He can hardly get the words out.*) Jerry's b-b-b-bad. You g-gotta talk to h-h-him.

TOM: What's the matter?

SONNY: D-don't tell him I t-told you.

SONNY *rides off. *TOM *turns the car and heads for the mill.*

Exterior: The Mill—Dawn

JERRY *sits on his motorbike, alone on the flat roof of an abandoned outbuilding, near the edge, which drops a hundred feet down to the railway line and the river. There are skid marks on the roof, as if he'd been circling around playing some bizarre form of Russian roulette, testing how close he could ride to the edge. He is looking across the river.*

Behind him we see the yard of his workshop and the tabernacle. TOM *is approaching him cautiously across the ramp to the roof. Behind him stand* SONNY *and* MONTANA, *watching anxiously.*

TOM *has taken in the suicide implication and moves slowly toward the motorbike. He finally hunkers down near* JERRY.

TOM: Jerry?

JERRY *stirs enough to indicate he heard, but for a long moment he doesn't respond. Then:*

JERRY: You believe he walked on the water?

TOM: I don't know how to believe it . . . but I guess there's no way not to—for one of *us*, right?

JERRY (*looks out on the dark river flowing by*): Funny . . . you came just in time. (*He turns the motorbike and rides back toward the mill across the ramp. As he rides past* SONNY *and* MONTANA:) Ain't you two got work to do? (*He disappears into the mill.*)

Interior: Tabernacle—A Little Later

TOM *enters through the plastic doors and stands by the central pillar. The tabernacle is much further along than it was before. The grids behind the reflecting hubcaps are in position, framing the statue of the Major. Colored "flags" of sacking are suspended in ceremonial positions. Candles are burning, and the melange of hubcaps shimmers in the half-light like armor.*

The lamb, in its pen, sleeps peacefully on straw before the altar. The crates that form the neat square of "pews" are in position.

JERRY *sits in complete stillness before the altar. The scene is somehow eerie and pathetic at the same time.*

TOM *walks quietly to a back pew.*

TOM: I have to hand it to you, it's beautiful. You really got yourself a church. People are gonna want to come here.

JERRY *seems to be in an agony of doubt. He starts shaking his head slowly and silently, then turns to* TOM, *the unlit altar behind his head.*

JERRY: I am unclean.

TOM (*lets this sit for a moment, then replies sympathetically*): Truthfully, kid . . . I been kind of wondering about that myself.

JERRY *looks at him.*

You know what they say—coke is high and smack is higher—but there's no high on God's earth like a true confession.

JERRY *stares ahead at Tom's meaning; it seems to expand*

toward some beckoning liberation. TOM *moves closer to him and sits within arm's length, speaking intimately.*

Been wanting to say this to you. . . . I ran your situation by an old friend of mine—retired federal judge, smart as a whip. He says if you'd see him and talk out an affidavit, Jer', sayin' how you tried to confess but the cops threw you out in the street . . . he's sure the feds would let you walk— for helpin' them clean out City Hall, y'know? Because the town's gotten evil, Jer', real horrendous. . . . You know that.

JERRY (*looks at* TOM *wide-eyed, as if awakening, then nods*): Oh, you got no idea . . .

TOM: About what?

JERRY: All the people Daniels used to pay . . .

TOM: Like who?

JERRY: Haggerty, Bellanca—everybody! . . . I mean every month! He used to brag about it!

TOM (*rising*): Well, that's behind you, Jerry. You've gotten through it. You understand me? You're through it! You've got a church of your own here. You've got something to say to people. And you've got a whole life ahead of you. You gotta cut free!

> JERRY *stares ahead, both excited and conflicted by a prospect of liberation.*

I'll stick with you. I'll be right there.

JERRY: Angie . . . know about this?

TOM: Me coming here? No. Why?

JERRY (*in an almost childlike plaint*): All I wanted was to talk to Daniels about buildin' my church . . . and he owed me money. But he wouldn't even open the goddamn door. . . . And he had like five locks.

TOM: I don't follow you, Jer' . . .

JERRY: Well, he'd always open for *her.*

TOM (*a stillness settling over his face, horror rising in his eyes*): Angela . . . was with you?

JERRY: I wasn't expecting to do anything, I swear.

TOM: So what'd you do? Hide until he opened the door?

JERRY: Yeah.

TOM: What'd she do?

JERRY (*puzzled*): I don't know.

TOM: She didn't go inside with you?

JERRY: I think so. I don't remember. I just lost my mind. He really pissed me off . . .

TOM: Why did she go with you?

JERRY: I asked her.

TOM (*with a hint of command, unable to bear this any longer*): Okay, come on! Let's go talk to the man now.

JERRY: Wait! What's going to happen to Angela?

TOM: Jerry, this is going to get her clear too. It's going to save her!

JERRY (*with a look of discovery on his face*): Right.

TOM: Let's go.

TOM *puts his arm around Jerry's shoulder.* JERRY, *finally free, allows* TOM *to lead him away.*

Exterior: Highway—Day

Jerry's bike crests a small rise on a winding highway, Tom's car behind him. JERRY *slows down a little to allow* TOM *to catch up, then waves his arm at* TOM *to follow faster.*

Interior: Tom's Car—Same Time

His face full of anticipation, sensing victory, TOM *watches* JERRY *speed ahead.*

Exterior: Highway—Moments Later

JERRY *is ahead. He comes to a sudden swerving stop.* TOM *has to brake to avoid him, but* JERRY *only draws up beside Tom's car, facing him through the window.*

JERRY: I'm beginning to feel good about this. I mean . . . I *feel* it!

JERRY *again waves* TOM *on to hurry. As Tom's car sets off,* JERRY *U-turns behind him and overtakes him with a roar.*

Interior: Tom's Car—Same Time

TOM *is full of anticipation as he follows behind the bike, but in a moment his look changes to concern.*

Exterior: Highway—Same Time

Tom's point of view: Jerry's bike is swerving from side to side, but under complete control. It is a joyous ride.

Close-up: The bike veers, Tom's car behind. Jerry's face grows jubilant, exhilarated. He switches off the engine, and the bike begins to coast. He raises his face to the sky. A solemn look of prayerful joy rises in him. He lifts his arms upward as though to embrace the sky, the sun flashing on his face.

Interior: Tom's Car—Same Time

Alarm is growing on his face, and he tries to speed up.

Exterior: Highway—Same Time

Close-up: JERRY *seems to be floating in a dream, his innocence returned, his guilt flying out of him, arms still in the air, eyes closed.*

Cresting another rise, we see that the bike is freewheeling down the hill. Tom's car begins to catch up. Time seems to stand still. Jerry's bike, now gliding toward a bend, narrowly misses an oncoming car.

Approaching a curve, JERRY, *still dreaming, is heading for an embankment. At the last moment, he seems to realize what is happening. He tries to save himself, but the bike flies over the embankment.*

Insert: Newspaper

The local paper, with blurred photos and the headline "Cult Leader Dies On Bike."

Interior: Tom's House—Morning

CONNIE *has the paper spread on the high kitchen counter,*

and she leans over it, holding her breakfast coffee cup. TOM, *grim-faced, is collecting papers from his desk, ready to go out.*

CONNIE: Well, he's in God's hands now.

TOM *nods.*

He was your whole case, wasn't he?

TOM: No. (*He puts on his overcoat.*) There's still an innocent man in jail.

CONNIE: What are you going to do?

TOM: I'm going to finish it.

CONNIE *nods.* TOM *starts to exit.*

CONNIE: Just don't buy her nightmares.

Exterior: Judge Murdoch's Estate—Woods—Day

TOM *and Judge* MURDOCH *are walking along a path through the misty woods of the Murdoch farm. The judge is in outdoor clothes and carries a beloved walking stick.*

TOM: So it makes her an accessory to a homicide, correct?

MURDOCH: I'd say so, yes.

TOM: But if I could get her to sign a statement that she saw Jerry kill Daniels, that would be new evidence, right? And Felix could get a new trial.

MURDOCH: But supposing she did more than get Jerry into that house? What if she helped him kill the doctor?

TOM: Jesus.

Murdoch takes a silver flask out of his pocket. He unscrews the top, which doubles as a jigger, pours a shot for himself, and offers the flask to Tom. *They drink,* Tom *hands back the flask.*

MURDOCH: I'm worried about you. Who knows what could pop out of the underbrush with a woman like this?

Tom: But the boy is innocent, Judge—

MURDOCH: He should never have been convicted! Those goddamn lawyers couldn't defend a nine-month-old baby against a charge of rape!

Tom: What do you think, is there some possible deal so she doesn't go to jail if she unloads?

MURDOCH: You're really not going to give up on this.

Tom: I can't.

They walk in silence for a moment. Tom *turns to the judge, embarrassed but insistent.*

Could I beg you to give her half an hour—just to see if there's some angle?

MURDOCH: Call Jean, make an appointment. Thirty minutes, no more.

Tom: Fantastic!

MURDOCH: Just remember, kid—the human race ate the apple. Reversing this case is not going to hang it back on the tree!

Interior: Seaside Restaurant—Dusk

It is a fish restaurant, quite middle-class, almost empty

now, out of season. There's a view of the ocean from the table.
ANGELA *is digging into a lobster.* TOM *studies the drink in
front of him.*

TOM: Angela . . .

*She glances up at him with a butter-smudged smile. Slight
pause.*

Jerry told me what went down the night he did it to
Daniels. You're an accessory to homicide.

ANGELA: I'd love a B-and-B.

He summons a WAITER.

TOM (*to* WAITER): B-and-B for the lady.

The WAITER *leaves. Another slight pause.*

This was what you were trying to cough up, wasn't it? . . .
From day one.

ANGELA: I'd love to go dancing. You want to?

TOM: Did you ever confess it to that priest? . . . No, huh?

Her silence concedes this.

Listen, I had a talk with Judge Murdoch. (*He pauses as the
WAITER sets a drink in front of* ANGELA *and leaves.*) He'd be
willing to see you, Ange.

A black look of alarmed suspicion is her reply.

You're in a situation, kid. Your eyewitness testimony places
Jerry at the scene a few minutes before the murder. It
would just about clear Felix.

ANGELA: And what happens to me?

Tom: That's why I think you ought to talk to the judge.

Angela: I want to go somewhere.

Tom: We are somewhere.

> Angela *moves to get up.*

Please, Ange . . . it's not going to go 'way.

Angela: Why isn't it?

> *She sees Tom's eyes—filled with pity for her, but also with a certain* direction—*and she hears the fearful absence of a reply from him. He reaches toward her with a calming hand.*

> *Exterior: Pier—Night*

> *We see an all but deserted resort, with boarded-up rides and ice cream stands—a small Coney Island off-season. The warped boards underfoot glisten after a rain. Tom and An-gela are walking separately, not touching: she emotionally trying to escape, he persistently hanging on. They hear a distant barking and halt, facing the sea.*

Angela: Dogs out there? They sound hurt.

Tom: No, that's seals, I think. Calling to each other.

Angela (*softened, enviously*): Huh! And right in the middle of the ocean.

> *They sit on a bench, still not touching. Angela turns to Tom with a tense attempt at a grin.*

You going to turn me in?

Tom: How could I turn you in even if I wanted to? My evidence died on a motorcycle.

ANGELA (*impatiently now*): Well, what's the deal, Tom, what's happening?

TOM: I think if you dictated a deposition stating that you got Victor to open the door for Jerry . . .

ANGELA: . . . I'd be an accessory to a murder.

TOM: Not necessarily, if Jerry forced you or tricked you, it was under duress. That's why I want you to get with the judge.

ANGELA: And what do I do when the rest of it starts coming up?

>   TOM *goes silent, stalemated.*

How does the great Dr. Daniels come to've known a bum like Jerry? That has to go straight to the drugs and the cops—and Angela's floatin' out there, feeding those seals.

TOM (*concedes, lowering his eyes*): Why did you call me in on this case, Angela?

ANGELA: To spring Felix. I thought maybe you could find some way . . . (*She breaks off.*)

TOM: . . . Without involving you.

>   *She concedes in silence.*

You couldn't bear carrying this anymore, is that it?

>   *She barely nods, eyes lowered.*

Funny, I keep trying to figure what it is that always pulls me back to you. It's your conscience. Which nobody is going to believe, but there it is.

>   *This statement of his respect for her draws a sob from* AN-

GELA, *but it may also be guilt for lying to him. She suddenly strides away down the pier, her conflict intolerable. He hurries after her.*

Honey! Wait! Angela! Listen to me!

He catches up with her. She is openly weeping.

ANGELA: Please don't turn me in!

TOM, *wracked, folds her into his arms, but no reassurance comes to his lips.*

Exterior: Pier—Night

TOM *and* ANGELA *are on the beach underneath the pier. The neon signs of hotels and hotdog stands glow behind them. She comes to a piling and leans on it, tense and exhausted. She is staring, avoiding his eyes. For a long moment nothing is said.*

ANGELA: The thing is . . . if I ever got on a witness stand, God knows what I might start saying.

TOM: Like what, honey?

ANGELA: Well, like . . . I might have made all that up about Charley. (*She looks directly at him for the first time.*) . . . I mean I'm not absolutely sure.

The question rises to his face—is she slyly using her illness to manipulate him, or is she really trying to avoid a catastrophe for them both in court?

TOM: No kidding.

ANGELA: I don't know. I'm almost sure of it, but suddenly every once in a while I . . . (*She breaks off, staring.*)

TOM: But you remember going to the doctor's house with Jerry.

ANGELA (*stares, trying to visualize*): I'm not . . . I'm not sure.

TOM (*feels a new skepticism but downs it*): No kidding.

ANGELA: I couldn't get up on a stand an' face Charley. I mean, God knows, maybe all I ever did with him was shake hands.

TOM: I saw the pictures, remember?

ANGELA: I don't know, maybe I dreamed it all.

TOM (*grabbing her arm*): I got a few things talking to Jerry.

ANGELA (*with the faintest hardening*): Jerry was brain-damaged. That wasn't the first time he tried to kill himself, you know.

TOM: Because he'd murdered Daniels? (*He grips her shoulders, his frustration boiling up in him.*) Nearly hacked his head off? (*He shouts.*) Damn near cut his heart out of his chest?

> *She tries to draw away, but he grips her.*

Nobody dreamed *that*, kid.

> *She tries to wrench free.*

You saw it all, didn't you! Went inside with him, didn't you? Is that it? You saw him try to cut his head off, is that what's driving you crazy?

> *She violently disengages, and his control begins to leave him as he senses that she knows more.*

What'd you, help hold him down, is that it? You held Daniels down for him? Angela!!

> *A most pleasurable, wild grin grows on her face.*

What're you laughing at? (*He shakes her violently.*) Stop laughing at me!

ANGELA: You realize what you're saying to me? You hear your own words? (*She screams into his face.*) I helped cut a man's head off? Do you hear your mouth!

He is stunned by the sudden insanity of the idea, for her indignation is very real.

Maybe now you get the feeling—do you?—that everything is possible and impossible at the same time, right? You feel it? This is what I live with all the time!

She sinks to the sand, exhausted. What to believe?— TOM *kneels, pulls her into his arms to comfort her.*

TOM: Honey, listen . . . I understand. You've got to talk to the judge. I know he'll come up with an idea. Just give it a try, what's to lose!

The pain of her uncertainty pierces him.

I love you, darlin'. I can't help it, I always will.

He draws her to him. His unguarded confession moves her, but the anxiety in her face remains.

Exterior: Judge Murdoch's Estate—Late Afternoon

Long shot: A wide and imposing view of the judge's house shows TOM *pulling into the driveway, with* ANGELA *beside him.*

Interior: Tom's Car—Same Time

As the car comes to a stop, ANGELA *touches her hair worriedly. She has dressed for the occasion.*

ANGELA: How do I look?

TOM: Great. Beautiful. (*He pats her thigh reassuringly.*) Come on. (*He gets out to open the car door for her.*)

Exterior: Outside the House—Same Time

TOM *and* ANGELA *walk toward the house.*

ANGELA: Tom? Can I do this alone? . . .

TOM: All right. But remember, he can only give you half an hour.

Interior: Judge Murdoch's House—Foyer—Same Time

Judge MURDOCH *opens the door in shirtsleeves and a cardigan, looking as though he's been working.*

MURDOCH: Hi, Tom. (*He shakes hands with* ANGELA.) How do you do, Mrs. Crispini.

ANGELA: Hello, sir.

MURDOCH: Come in, come in. (*He gestures in the direction of his study.*)

Angela goes ahead, but Tom stays at the threshold with Murdoch.

TOM: When should I come back?

MURDOCH: Don't bother. I'll hear her out, and Billy can drive her home.

TOM: Judge—I don't have to tell you how grateful I am!

MURDOCH: Forget it. (*He shuts the door behind him.*)

Exterior: Judge Murdoch's House—Same Time

About to get into his car in the driveway, TOM *looks back at the house and through a low leaded window sees* MURDOCH *removing Angela's coat, throwing his head back with a laugh at some remark she has apparently made.* TOM *grins with pride in her courage, gets into his car, and drives off.*

Exterior: Tom's House—Next Day—Late Afternoon

Tom's car is there. Connie's car pulls up, and she gets out and goes into the house, carrying her briefcase and groceries.

Interior: Tom's House—Same Time

As CONNIE *comes into the kitchen,* TOM *comes out of the bedroom in his bathrobe, still groggy with sleep, apparently just awakened by her arrival.*

TOM: My God, what time is it?

CONNIE: About half past four.

TOM: What!!! (*He stumbles to his desk, where the message light on his answering machine is blinking rapidly.*)

CONNIE: You slept all day. The load must be off your back.

TOM *has pushed the playback button, and as he hears the following messages, he's searching his address book.*

RECORDED VOICE: (JEAN, *after the beep*): Tom, this is Jean in Judge Murdoch's office, he'd like you to call him right away.

TOM *punches the judge's number; the messages continue as he talks.*

RECORDED VOICE (MURDOCH, *after the beep*): Tom, this is Harry Murdoch. Give me a call.

TOM (*into phone*): Judge! It's Tom. (*He turns off the answering machine.*) What's happening?

MURDOCH (*voice-over, through phone*): Tom, I'm in a meeting. But listen, she's got a remarkable story, and I've decided to get into it myself.

TOM: That is *great*!

MURDOCH (*voice-over*): It's outrageous! Did you know Haggerty actually batted her around?

TOM: She told you all that?

MURDOCH (*voice-over, interrupting*): Now look, I've sent her out of state just in case somebody tries to get at her . . .

TOM (*surprised*): Where is she?

MURDOCH (*voice-over, ignoring the question*): Tom, this is a job for a lawyer. I've got this under control. I want you to sit back and let me take it from here.

TOM: Sure! Fantastic!

MURDOCH: I'll be in touch by the end of the week.

> MURDOCH *hangs up.* TOM *puts down the phone, and* CONNIE *hands him a glass of juice. He doesn't notice her for the moment. Then he speaks.*

TOM: Something's happened, Connie . . . finally! Imagine! She told the judge the real story!

CONNIE: Well, that's good news . . .

TOM: I mean, the man was *outraged!* And when he gets going, he'll take those punks to the cleaners. That guy's Ted Williams on a good day. He'll murder those bums.

CONNIE: Tom, I'm happy for you.

TOM: Thanks for hanging in there, Conn . . .

She lightly swats his hand away.

Exterior: Courthouse Square—Day

TOM, *out of breath, is running up the hill from the direction of the courthouse toward Judge Murdoch's office.*

JEAN, *Murdoch's secretary, is leaving to go home. She's just unlocking her car as he runs up.*

JEAN (*sure he knows this already*): The judge wants to see you on Friday, Tom.

TOM: I got the message. Look, I really need to reach Mrs. Crispini. And I know you can tell me where she is. Now, how about it, Jean?

JEAN: You know better than to ask me that, Tom.

TOM: Jean, I've got to know what's going on!

JEAN (*sympathetically, after hesitating*): Well . . . I really shouldn't tell you this, but . . . you know the judge who presided at Felix Daniels' trial?

TOM: Yablonsky! What about him?

JEAN: The judge is having lunch with him on Thursday.

Tom's face lights up. He gives her a quick kiss.

TOM: Jean, I love you!

Exterior: Tom's House—Pasture—Day

Close up: TOM *is exultant as he hurls a stick across the pasture. The stick tumbles through the air and finally bounces on the ground. Tom's Labrador dashes up, seizes the stick in his teeth, and romps back to* TOM, *who cuddles the dog happily.*

Exterior: Judge Murdoch's Estate—Day

Preparations for a large party are going on as TOM *comes up to the house. The front door is open.* JEAN *and servants are setting out chairs at the rented tables arranged on the terrace, which is now covered with a bright striped awning.* JEAN *gestures to* TOM, *implying* MURDOCH *is in, and* TOM *goes on inside.*

Interior: Judge Murdoch's House—Stairs—Exercise Room—Shower—Day

TOM *enters a hallway from the stairs, knocks on a door.*

MURDOCH (*off screen*): Come on in!

TOM *steps into the judge's exercise room. There's a stationary bicycle, a Nautilus-type machine, and* MURDOCH, *in his shorts, on a rowing machine.*

Well, I've just got your boy out on bail.

TOM (*electrified*): What!

MURDOCH (*nods*): I've decided to take on the case myself.

TOM: My God, Judge!

MURDOCH (*stops rowing and gives a faint, proud smile*): There's no question the State held back exculpatory evidence. It's a technicality, but it'll get him a new trial. And who's gonna fight it now this Jerry kook is dead?

TOM: You are unbelievable! Then she told you the whole story, huh?

> MURDOCH *starts rowing again.* TOM, *eager for the kill, grins vengefully as he leans in closer.*

This trial is gonna bring the whole thing crashing down— Haggerty, Bellanca—the whole damn police department!

> TOM *breaks off as he sees that* MURDOCH *has not been reacting as expected to this idea.* MURDOCH *looks at him with the deepest gravity.*

MURDOCH: I've sprung Felix, Tom—that'll have to be the end of it.

TOM (*astounded, incredulous*): What do you mean, Judge?

MURDOCH (*with something like indignation now*): I have sprung Felix, and that will be the end of the matter.

TOM: But didn't she tell you? Haggerty took payoffs, and so did Bellanca.

MURDOCH (*forcefully*): Now, Tom, you heard me . . .

TOM: You haven't got the picture, Judge! She could blow the roof off the city!

> MURDOCH *just pulls off his shorts, steps into the shower, and turns on the water, leaving the door open.*

MURDOCH (*decisively*): The woman has been through enough, Tom! And I must tell you, I think you've been damned rough on her!

TOM (*bewildered*): Me!!

MURDOCH: This is a sensitive human being, a . . . a *deep* human being! I will not allow her to be tortured any further by this case!

TOM (*seeing the incredible sexual situation*): My God, Harry, you can't be tellin' me that you . . .

MURDOCH: Felix is out, and that's it! She can't cure the world! (*He closes the shower door.*)

Exterior: Judge Murdoch's House—Day

TOM *comes out a side door, walking into more party preparations: musicians coming in with their instruments and caterers setting up an outdoor bar. Suddenly a second-floor window toward the back of the house is flung open, and Judge* MURDOCH *leans out and calls after Tom.*

MURDOCH: Tom! You deserve a lot of credit for this, and I'll make sure the press hears about that!

MURDOCH *shuts the window.* TOM *keeps walking.*

Exterior: Judge Murdoch's Lawn—Guesthouse—Early Evening

As TOM *makes his way down the lawn toward his car, he passes a guesthouse. He hears a tapping and a muffled voice, and turning, sees* ANGELA *beckoning at a window. He goes to the door of the house, which immediately opens, and he enters. She is absolutely delighted to see him. She wears a robe.*

Interior: Guesthouse—Evening

ANGELA *is all ready for the party except for her dress, which is hanging on the bathroom door. Just before* TOM *enters, she locks the French windows and draws the curtains.*

ANGELA: Tom! Where you been?

TOM: Where *I* been?

ANGELA: We got Felix out, can you believe it? (*She kisses* TOM, *closes the door.*) I got the judge to send a car for him—he'll be here for the party. (*She puts on her bathrobe.*) Want some white wine? Can you imagine when Charley Haggerty sees him!

She pours a drink, then draws him into the room. From the main house a pianist is heard warming up.

Isn't this some place Harry's got here? He's such a marvelous human being ... and what a brain! I mean, it's fantastic what he's done. This way everybody wins!

TOM: ... Almost, yeah.

ANGELA: Why! Felix is out, what more do you want?

TOM (*with an ironical grin despite his seriousness*): "This case goes to the top of the mountain!" I thought I heard you say that once upon a time.

She turns away, and he reaches over to turn her to him.

Well, this is the top of the mountain, kid. With what you know we could have bombed hell out of this town, we really could. Or was anything like that *ever* in your mind?

Again she tries to turn away.

In other words, Felix is out and the monkey's off your back

and everything else stays exactly the same, and it doesn't
bother you for one split second, does it. What a horse's ass,
huh? (*He laughs.*)

ANGELA: Don't say that.

TOM: So what's next? You climb in the hammock with
Haggerty—or any other gorilla who has something you
might happen to want?

*She smashes him across the face, and he automatically grabs
her. He raises his hand to hit her and just stops himself.*

Christ, now you got *me* doing it!

He is at an impasse. Neither knows what to say.

ANGELA (*serious*): You know what they're like. They'd have
destroyed me.

He looks into her eyes, conceding the simple, hated truth.

TOM: Yeah. I guess I was expecting too much. (*He moves to
leave.*)

ANGELA: We saved a man, Tommy—that's not nothing.

TOM (*nodding*): It's true. (*Again he moves to leave.*)

ANGELA (*daring to touch his face*): Please . . . I'll always love
you! You can't stop being my friend.

We hear the sound of guests outside.

Exterior: Judge Murdoch's Lawn Party—Evening

*The party orchestra starts to play "Some Enchanted Eve-
ning."*

Judge MURDOCH *is greeting and chatting with some guests,
among them* BELLANCA *and some* DETECTIVES. MURDOCH

*moves away from this group toward the guesthouse. He knocks
on the French door.*

Interior: Guesthouse—Evening

ANGELA *has removed her robe. She is putting on her dress.*

MURDOCH (*off screen*): Angela?

ANGELA (*sotto*): Would you mind going out the back?

TOM (*starting to laugh*): Why?

MURDOCH (*off screen*): Angela! Are you in there?

ANGELA: I'm coming, dear! Be with you in a minute! (*Sotto to*
TOM:) Come! (*She draws him toward the rear door of the
house.*)

TOM (*laughing*): What are we hiding for?

MURDOCH (*off screen*): Why have you locked the door?

ANGELA: Please, he's very old-fashioned in some ways, he'll
be upset. He's absolutely crazy about me! (*She pulls the back
door open and tries to push* TOM *out.*)

MURDOCH *has started pounding his shoulder against the
door. She calls to him over her shoulder.*

ANGELA: Just a minute!

MURDOCH (*off screen*): Open the door.

ANGELA (*meaning it this time*): WAIT!

TOM *catches the edge in her voice. It amuses him.*

ANGELA (*sotto*): Thanks. And bless you, Tommy!

TOM (*ironically*): And "please go," right?

She nods her head.

TOM: Go on, let him in. (*He exits, closing the door.*)

Interior: Guesthouse—Evening

Tom's point of view: ANGELA *lets* MURDOCH *in as* TOM *leaves.*

MURDOCH: Everything all right?

ANGELA: Yes, fine, fine. I was in the bathroom. I didn't hear you. Would you like a magazine? *Time? Newsweek?* (*She hands him a magazine.*) I'll be just a minute. I have to put some finishing touches. Sit. Sit. That's a beautiful suit. (*She walks toward the window, through which* TOM *can be seen outside. She gives him a look.*)

MURDOCH: You certainly are something to look at, and I mean *something.*

Exterior: Guesthouse—Evening

TOM, *passing the window, stops to watch the scene within the guesthouse.*

Interior: Guesthouse—Evening

ANGELA *is laughing joyously at some remark of the judge's. Her outstretched hand, nearest* TOM, *makes a delicate wave of farewell.* MURDOCH *looks at her adoringly.*

MURDOCH: Go on, now, get dressed.

As she turns toward the bathroom, she is facing TOM *for an instant. She gives him a kind of lost smile and a shrug, as though to say, "I have to survive, forgive me, dear . . ." Freeze frame.*

Exterior: Lawn Party—Evening

TOM *is coming from the guesthouse. He would like to slink away unseen, but he has to cross the lawn to reach his car.*

Now, at the farthest edge of the crowd, he spots MURDOCH *and* ANGELA, *who are just joining the party from the direction of the guesthouse.* MURDOCH *is shaking hands. She is laughing and enjoying herself immensely.*

TOM *turns away and leaves the party behind, moving toward the line of expensive cars where his old car is parked. He hears a voice calling.*

FELIX: Mr. O'Toole!

TOM *turns to see* FELIX *hurrying up to him from the party. Father* MANCINI *is with him, beaming proudly.*

TOM: Felix! Lookin' great! How's it going?

FELIX *is barbered now, in a good suit much too big for him, but the prison pallor is still on him. He embraces* TOM *emotionally.*

A new number from the orchestra is drowning out their dialogue— FELIX *is obviously thanking* TOM, *who responds warmly.* TOM *finally shakes hands again and gets into his car.* FELIX *stands there waving to him as he drives away.*

We stay with TOM *as he drives. Slowing at the end of the driveway to turn onto the road, he sees a van arriving with a campaign sign on top: a photo of* HAGGERTY, *with "Haggerty for Senator" below it.*

TOM *sets his jaw and drives past the van. He jams a tape button and overwhelms everything with music, seeming to breathe easier, in cleaner air.*

The camera elevates, taking in the whole town on the judge's lawn as Tom's old car drives away.

Exterior: Highbury—Evening

We see TOM *driving, his beloved music almost making him smile, but the mystery of it all remains in his eyes.*

Tom's point of view: We see the immemorial life of the small city: firemen polishing their great machines in the firehouse, shopkeepers closing up for the evening, women hurrying home with groceries, the Main Street intersection and the traffic . . .

Tom's car crosses the bridge out of Highbury, heading back into the countryside.